"Four Questions of Creativity"

(Keys to a creative life)

By Piers Worth Ph.D.

Order this book online at www.trafford.com
or email orders@trafford.com

Most Trafford titles are also available at major online book retailers.

I gratefully acknowledge the permission of Professor Mihalyi Csikszentmihalyi
to reproduce quotations from his writings on 'Flow' in Chapter 1.

The picture on the cover of this book is an infrared photograph taken by Dr Andrew Machon,
used with gratitude, with permission as a wonderful illustration of both creativity and emergence.
More of his work can be viewed on www.andrewmachon.com

The photographs contained in the preface and epilogue are used under license from IStockphoto.com

Printed in Victoria, BC, Canada.

ISBN: 978-1-4269-2544-3

Library of Congress Control Number: 2010902579

*Our mission is to efficiently provide the world's finest, most comprehensive book publishing
service, enabling every author to experience success. To find out how to publish your book, your
way, and have it available worldwide, visit us online at www.trafford.com*

Trafford rev. 06/08/2010

 www.trafford.com

North America & international
toll-free: 1 888 232 4444 (USA & Canada)
phone: 250 383 6864 ◆ fax: 812 355 4082

Table of Contents

Preface

"Neither a lofty degree of intelligence nor imagination nor both together go to the making of a genius.   Love, love, love – that is the soul of genius."
(Wolfgang Amadeus Mozart)

This book was born out of a wish to understand how someone might be creative, and maintain this capacity productively and happily as they aged.

This is a culmination of a fascination I have had with creativity that has now lasted most of my adult life.   As a younger person I would look at a beloved artist friend with fascination: how could she work as she did?   How could she have the life that she did, so focused on art?   How could she be continuing this work (new forms of creativity and art) at an age (70+) when most people appeared (to me at least) to be doing quite the reverse?   In my eyes, when I have seen this quality in her and others, it appears to be individuals living a life of their choice and with skills and actions that express deeply who they are.   Seeing this in another person, I believed I was sensing energy, a resonance and a courage that I did not have in my life.   Bluntly, feeling this was not the sort of person *I* was, I wanted to learn more of it, and to know how I might incorporate this in my life, particularly as I got older.

The fascination with creativity led, eventually, to my undertaking a PhD exploring how this developed in individual lives over their lifespan.   I completed that work in 2001 and have spent a lot of the intervening time deeply involved with its implications.   In hindsight, I felt I saw individuals move through the process illustrated in this diagram (overleaf).

The Development of a 'Creative' Life?

Relationship with an area of skill or work

Role models
and
Influential adults

Mentors

Developing creative working practices

Patterns of creative productivity over time

I have tried to weave what I learnt from my PhD into my life, and to support creativity's unfolding in the lives of others: students I have worked with in a university setting and clients in my work as a psychotherapist, lecturer and management coach.

In hindsight, I realise there were four key questions that I was trying to answer in my PhD research (that reflect the process in the diagram above.) My goal in writing this book has been to answer those questions.

1. What is 'creativity'?
2. How do I become creative?
3. What is mentoring in this context?
4. How might creativity change as we age?

These questions, to me, sum up the pathway through which we find and develop creative expression over time. I believe that, if any of us can answer these questions, we are closer to a capacity or practice of a creative life.

Several audiences might be interested in this approach.

• These questions of creativity may be of importance to a serious 'student', both in the areas of human development, and how our individual lives may unfold for the better, e.g. psychology, counselling, psychotherapy or human resources.

- Each chapter is 'free-standing' and can be read alone, albeit that they have a cumulative message if read together. They are intended to offer ideas and perspectives that might resource your own journey or that of others through some or all of these questions of creativity. Equally, sections within the chapters might also be read alone if they are subjects of particular interest or concern. Each chapter points readers to choice and action.

- I believe each chapter also offers new perspectives for an academic in this domain of study. I believe the book can contribute to the understanding of teachers, parents, managers, human resources or organisation development professionals and coaches, counsellors and psychotherapists in how to recognise and nurture creativity.

Each chapter acts as a guided walk through one of the four questions. I open each chapter (or in some cases each major section) with a summary of key points. The main body of the chapter is a detailed review of literature and ideas associated with the question. I have woven into these discussions detail and practices I learnt from my research. I close each chapter with reflective questions which may guide readers towards change.

The style of writing is both personal and academic. The academic tradition involves citing one's sources of ideas and literature within the text. Because this work is also aimed different groups of 'informed readers' I am pointing to references via end notes at the rear of the book, and onward to detailed references at the rear of the book in order not to break the reader's flow of attention.

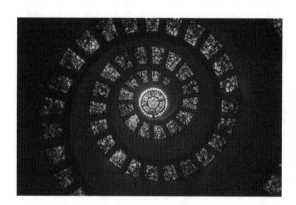

A key premise of this book is what I term the Creative Spiral. I started to use the phrase because of the stories I have heard about creative lives. I found myself believing, seeing that the opportunity to find, develop or change our creativity occurs at many ages through our lifetime. Our lives have structural elements – school days, starting an occupation, becoming a 'professional', the mid-life period, middle age, retirement – each of which offer us opportunities to choose and re-choose a life path. A decision made at one point can be re-made at another. Choices that were *not* taken at one time can be revisited in another time. The 'spiral' will return us to that possibility, albeit at a different time and circumstances. Therefore it may never be 'too late'. Choices can be changed, or re-made. We find our own 'voice' and more of it. We loosen the grip of social pressure on our work, each allowing us more freedom that we previously experienced. The chance to 'find' creativity occurs at many ages.

At the same time I would like this text to be a resource in the emergent field of 'Positive Psychology'. The mixture of personal and academic writing, and the reflective exercises, follows the style of presentation in some recent positive psychology texts. It is a description and exploration of one of the most positive and meaningful experiences of our humanity, what has become termed a 'signature strength' – creativity.

Catherine Yarrow was the artist and friend from my early adulthood who brought me to these questions and this path. Ron Long was a boss of mine nearly twenty years ago, and also one of the most profoundly creative people I have ever met. In having the willingness to employ me and others because we *couldn't* do our jobs, and because we would grow into them, he gave me the example and courage to follow my questions, and many new paths. My gratitude and debt too these two people are enduring and expressed every day of my life. They and their creativity have been fundamental influences on my life and who I have become.

Many dear friends and colleagues have kept me company on this journey. I want to express both gratitude and love to the following, for their contribution to my understanding and expression of this material. Alphabetically, by surname: Jane Archutowska, Mel Ephgrave, Steve Fomin, Penny Gill; Lois Graessle, Jane Henry, Liz Jordan, David and Paddy Lilley, Helena Linnett, Andrew Machon, Michael Manthorpe, John Martin, Tony O'Connell, Peter and Sherryl Scott, Scott Tower, and Buntie Wills.

My first opportunity to teach university students occurred recently at Buckinghamshire New University. The 08/09 cohort of students on psychology, psycho-social and criminological psychology courses were a joy to be with. They were as much my 'teacher' as I was theirs, and I thank them for what I learned in their company.

Chapter 1: What is 'Creativity'?

"… the heart's creative wisdom has a more important message than anything else, and our task in life is to realise that message". Naomi Wolf (2006).

Introduction

Whomever I work with, be they psychotherapy clients, students I mentor, or managers I coach, there is a constant and recurring theme. They have a yearning to discover a part of themselves, a way of expression and living that they believe is a unique reflection of who they truly are. It comes across, to someone listening, as a 'hunger'. My experience argues that when individual creative expression is found, we become more defined, stronger in identity and more true to ourselves. The essence, hope and intention of this book are to trace the journey of that yearning and expression.

There are many words in our language and our society that can describe the characteristics or experiences of this way of living fully, self-expression and a well-lived life. Yet within these, I believe this 'yearning' relates to three areas which recur to the serious questioner, reader or student of these issues. They are:

- Self-actualisation.
- Creativity.
- 'Flow'.

My proposition is that these three areas are inextricably linked, and overlap, each expressing an aspect of personal development. To me, self-actualisation is the 'yearning', creativity is the form of expression, and flow is its expression in action.

The central theme of this book is 'creativity'. To understand creativity I believe it is appropriate to place it within in the bigger picture of these two other topics, in part to help the reader navigate towards creativity, and also because I consider them each to be expressions of a similar theme in human experience – living more fully, completely and with vitality in our lives. If we choose to explore any one of these, I believe we are potentially on a path to the others.

Initially I saw them as three distinct yet related areas, potentially responding to three implied questions:

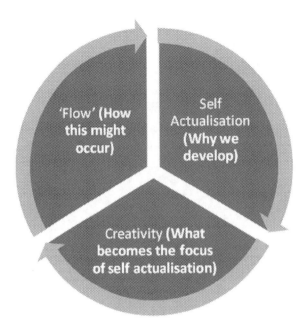

As I wrote and explored, I reached a different sense, of three areas that at times are one. My belief is that in its depth, creativity involves an expression or manifestation of each of these areas; something within us that is an expression of our full potential and the happiness that comes with an absorption in its experience. There is a centre-ground where all three are one; yet each may also be individual and distinct in appearance and content, separate from the others.

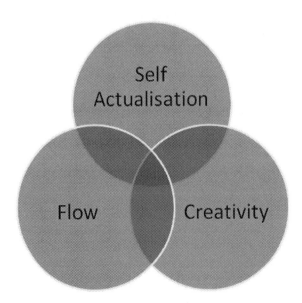

In my exploration I began to see self-actualisation as potentially 'why' we may seek to develop ourselves; creativity as perhaps 'what' we may do or express in order to reach it; and flow as 'how' we may do it.

What does 'creativity' mean to you?

Before summarising the literature in this 'domain'[1] of study, I encourage you to 'relate' to creativity, to reflect on questions that orientate you to this experience. Become familiar with these questions personally, even if you are reading this text in support of your work with others.

- What does 'creativity' mean to you?
- Where do you perceive or experience creativity?
- When?
- How?
- How do you react to the idea that these qualities or characteristics might also be found in other areas of your life as well?
- What activities give you pleasure or joy?
- In what activities do you experience time as 'stopping'?
- Why do you take part in these activities?
- What motivates you to do so?

In the review that follows I will first summarise the nature and characteristics of 'self-actualisation'. I will then offer a definition of 'creativity' and explore how research and writing in this domain offers arguments on its form and place in our lives. I move on with a review of 'flow' which I consider to mirror the characteristics of self-actualising and creative experiences in action. I close the chapter with a review of why the choice of these paths is important to us, and the potential contribution of the new perspective or discipline of 'positive psychology' within this search.

Self-actualisation

Summary of key points:
Self-actualisation occurs as we move towards the " full-use and exploitation of (our) talents, capabilities and potentialities".

Self-actualisation may represent a biological capacity to grow and express ourselves. I speculate that it may be an expression of Darwin's evolution in action.

Maslow argues that self-actualisation was a matter of degree, rather than 'all or nothing'.

Descriptions of 'self-actualisation' might seem to imply perfection. Yet Maslow was also specific that we might seek to express self-actualisation while still retaining our characteristic humanity, flawed though it may be.

Maslow saw creativity as a fundamental expression of self-actualisation. He described creativity as an attitude or approach that could affect all activities of life.

Self-actualisation comes after the fulfilment of other needs such as safety and security, respect and love. Maslow and Carl Rogers both implied self-actualisation arose in an environment where an individual felt accepted, respected or loved.

Self-actualisation features in the humanistic tradition of psychology and was introduced by Abraham Maslow [2]. It is an optimistic and positive perspective which sees within each of us an impulse towards growth. Self-actualisation happens as the individual moves towards "actualisation of potentialities, full potentialities, towards peak experiences" [3] and "... the full use and exploitation of talents, capabilities and potentialities" [4]. Maslow saw self-actualisation as a matter of "degree" rather than an "all-or-none" condition" [5].

When I think of the way others speak to me in a hungering, yearning way for an undiscovered form of expression, I believe I am hearing the urge to self-actualise, and an almost biologically-driven intensity to do so.

For Maslow, self-actualisation was the "ultimate goal of human life" and, he proposed, it appears at a peak of a hierarchy of needs or motives. These covered two groups, 'deficiency motives' and 'being motives'. These are (from base to peak):

1. Physiological needs (hunger and thirst).
2. Safety needs (a stable and predictable environment)
3. Love and belongingness needs (affection from others; need to be with others rather than alone).
4. Esteem needs (superiority, respect, self-respect).
5. Self-actualisation.

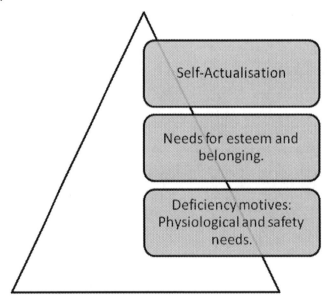

'Self-actualisation' is the highest level of this pyramid of needs. The needs are organised in a "relative potency" – the stronger needs appear earlier [6]. Maslow's view was that until an individual's basic needs were met the higher needs would not be prominent. Therefore, each of the higher levels defers to the lower and their satisfaction [7].

Maslow and Carl Rogers both implied that actualising individuals were supported or nurtured by an environment where they experienced acceptance, respect and love. [8]

Maslow saw self-actualisation as a motive emerging later in life and, implicitly, when physiological and social needs of life are in some measure 'met'. Developments in society and western economies since Maslow wrote 40 years ago might lead us to expect that needs lower in the hierarchy may be established as met relatively early for many people now, leaving large numbers of us with new needs for fulfilment in esteem and self-actualisation [9].

Maslow and Rogers both argued that this tendency to actualisation operated continuously, and drew us towards our development and enhancement, a personal differentiation and increasing mental or psychic complexity [10].

Mihalyi Csikszentmihalyi [11] suggests that there is a consensus among psychologists since Maslow's time of writing that this hierarchy represents a path through which individuals "develop their concept of who they are, and what they want to achieve in life". We focus initially on physiological security. When this is secure, we move our focus to the social community of which we are part, their values, norms and standards, and how we may feel part and secure amongst them. Self-actualisation is a step towards an individuality, inner authority and expression. This differentiates us from the collective of which we have become part, yet its expression may, conceivably, become a means by which we provide a service or an example to those around us [12]. In more recent literature on 'Positive Psychology' self-actualisation is connected with the 'eudaimonic approach' to well-being, suggesting that following activities that develop our individual potential is a primary source of happiness[13].

Maslow described his study of self-actualising individuals as personal, albeit structured and considered. He saw its implications for positive psychological health as so important that he proceeded on this basis, and implied the hope that further studies could follow.

There are further examples of life span developmental psychology, in the work of George Vaillant and Daniel Levinson, [14] that illustrate this unfolding in the stories of individuals and their gradual finding of personal 'voice' and aspirations.

While the writing on self-actualisation seems to imply human perfection, Maslow acknowledged that no individual was 'perfect '[15]. Maslow considered an empirical case had been made "for the presence within the human being of a tendency toward, or need for growing in a direction that can be summarised in general as self-actualisation or psychological health"[16].

Maslow saw self-actualisation as a matter of "degree" rather than an "all-or-none" condition, which he felt allowed a researcher to search biographies of creative, or any other individuals, for episodes of self-actualisation through peak or growth experiences

The words and phrases used by Maslow to describe self-actualisation include problem-centring, autonomy, peak experiences and creativity[17]. Other authors have used a plethora of terms to describe the self-actualising state: for example, "reality-centred, being comfortable alone but also being able to enjoy deep personal relationships, autonomy, positive non-conformity, a sense of humour, humility, a strong sense of ethics, creativity (…) and an acceptance of self and others"[18]. Maslow appears to have considered that all self-actualised subjects were creative.

Maslow saw creativity in a distinct manner. He wrote "creativity is a universal characteristic of all people studied and observed", "the creativeness appears in some of our subjects not in the usual forms of writing books, composing music or producing artistic objects, but rather may be much more humble." It is an expression of a healthy personality. Creativity "is projected out upon the world or touches whatever activity the person is engaged in". "Whatever one does can be done with a certain attitude, a certain spirit that arises out of the nature of the character of the person performing the act." "I learned to apply the word creative ... not only to products but also to people in a characterological way, and to activities and process and attitudes [19]. This attitude or style is described as displaying a movement from "...relative fixity to fluidity" in our personality and way of living [20].

Maslow proceeded to define creativity in the context of this subject in two separate ways. "... I found it necessary to distinguish "special talent creativeness" from "self-actualising creativeness" which sprang much more directly from the personality, which showed itself widely in the ordinary affairs of life ..." (ibid.: p159) [21]. I would argue that at times these two forms of creativity are different, and for some individuals encountered in my PhD research they can be the same, e.g. the special talent can be the individual's means of self-actualising.

Other writers, following Maslow, have added other perspectives and definitions to self-actualisation. Murphy 'et al' [22] saw self-actualisation "as being identified with integration, psychological health, individuation, autonomy, creativity and productivity. Self-actualisation is the ultimate goal of man who constantly tends towards growth". These authors perceived Maslow as describing creativity "as one way of expressing self-actualisation". This is a perspective reflected in Anna Craft's writing[23] – self-actualisation as a means of bringing one's own ideas and potentiality into another form, e.g. via creative activity.

Manheim[24] saw "the distinguishing mark of the self-actualising person is that she/he has more frequent and more intense experiences of peak moments than the average person". Maslow saw creativity as a route or gateway to peak experiences, a proposal that links both to the flow state, described later.

Reflective question:
Do you recognise in yourself a pull or a drive towards self-actualisation? A tendency to become your potential? An urge to expand, extend, develop and mature; to activate all your capacities?

These ideas suggest that creativity is a reflection of self-actualisation, and a means by which it is expressed. Let us now turn to explore the nature of creativity.

Creativity

If self-actualisation is the hunger or drive for expression, my interpretation is many reach for creativity as a form or medium through which to express themselves.

Summary of key points:
'Creativity' may be defined many ways. A definition that has become widely accepted is: "... it is both a novel and appropriate, useful, correct or valuable response to the task at hand".

This definition or description of creativity may be applied to a person, process, product or environment.

There is some argument in academic literature about where creativity may be found. I believe and maintain creativity may be encountered in everyday life as well as a particular talent or area of work.

Creative skills take time to develop. The length of time needed will be dependent on individual motivation and aspiration.

'Everyday creativity' might be seen as an attitude and skill that supports our response to and adjustment towards a changing environment.

I speculate that creativity develops within us individually, and grows or evolves towards something seen in a social context (see the continuum of creativity described in this section.)

All creativity occurs in some form of social context. This may be as simple as our being drawn as individuals to an established skill and the ways in which it is learnt and used. Or, for example, it may be parents, supporting a child in developing a skill, facing the practical and emotional tasks of creating these opportunities.

My experience supports the argument that, when we find some individual form of creativity, we become more defined, stronger in identity and time we devote to ourselves.

When I work with individuals and the discussion turns to creativity the reaction is almost always that this is a term that is hard to define, refers to the arts, sciences, and 'exceptional' people, not those of us who live in 'everyday' life. Yet Maslow's work, described above, argues that creativity has a strong presence in everyday life.

When you review academics writing and discussing this area of study you might also believe it can be a complex, even confusing area with many disagreements or 'threads' to the discussion. In an attempt to make these discussions and definitions accessible, I will examine the following topics:

- Definitions of creativity.
- Whether creativity is a 'special talent' and 'domain specific' creativity, or can also be 'everyday creativity?
- The influence of the social context on creativity.

Definitions of Creativity

A common starting point to enable us to define creativity is to examine its characteristics. Different definitions, offered by a range of academics and researchers in a milestone publication some years ago, share similar features, as the following range of examples illustrates:

Gruber & Wallace (1999: p94)   "The creative product must be new and must be given value according to some external criteria".

Martindale (1999: p137)   "A creative idea is one that is both original and appropriate for the situation in which it occurs".

Lumsden (1999: p153)   "Creativity is a kind of capacity to think up something new that people find significant".

Feist (1999: p274)	"... novel and adaptive solutions to problems".
Lubart (1999: p339)	"... the ability to produce work that is novel and appropriate".
Boden (1999: p351)	"... the generation of ideas that are both novel and valuable".
Feldman et al (1994: p1)	"... the achievement of something remarkable and new, something which transforms and changes a field of endeavour in a significant way".
Amabile (1996: p35)	**"... it is both a novel and appropriate, useful, correct or valuable response to the task at hand".**

I have highlighted the last definition because it has become so widely used. The phrasing of a majority of these definitions could apply to many settings. There continues to be an argument or split within academic creativity literature as to whether it refers to the 'exceptional' act, or whether it can be used more broadly, such as for everyday life. Later in this discussion I will describe the argument for 'everyday creativity' and argue that these definitions of creativity may also apply in this area as well.

The common theme within these definitions is novelty or originality combined with utility or value. These definitions also reflect a pattern of defining creativity by products, the characteristics of the outcome, whether an object or an idea – but not exclusively so. Many researchers have also focused on the "creative person", the "creative process" and/or the "creative press" or environments that originated the creative product or outcome[25]. In a description that is a personal favourite of mine, Frank Barron[26] illustrates how the person, process and product have become used in providing definitions of creativity. He writes:

"Creativity is the ability to respond adaptively to the needs for new approaches and new products. It is essentially the ability to bring something new into existence purposefully, though the process may have unconscious, or subliminally conscious, as well as fully conscious components. ... The "something new" is usually a product resulting from a process initiated by a person. These are therefore the three modes in which creativity may most easily be studied. The defining properties of these new products, processes, and persons are their originality, their aptness, their validity, their adequacy in meeting a need."

The primary focus I take in this writing is on the creative 'process' or 'product', yet the belief I hold is that this reflects, at the same time, the creative person.

I have found myself speculating if 'creativity', whether person, process or product, is a form of play. Perhaps this flexibility, the willingness to place different aspects in new relationships in seeking new outcomes is play in an alternative form. Natalie Rogers, the daughter of Carl Rogers, the psychologist, cites Carl Jung as suggesting no creative work comes into being without play or imagination in some form. Maybe creativity is also an aspect of our being that may keep us flexible or less rigid as we age? However challenging 'creativity' may be, I realised that all the creative individuals I know would describe 'work as play'. Keep this possibility or speculation in mind as you reflect on what follows.

'Special talent' creativity? 'Domain specific' creativity? Or 'everyday' creativity? Or all of them?

As someone who believes creative expression is so core to our humanity and to every individual, I feel a level or frustration at having to argue this level of definition.   Yet I believe it has a purpose in defining a locality in which different forms of creativity may be seen.

Keith Sawyer[27] offers the student or general reader a *tour de force* in his review of creativity. He suggests that, until the 1980s, the primary focus of study of creativity was exceptional acts, and activity in the arts and sciences.   My own observation is that this focus of attention remained well into the 1990s at least.   Academic creativity literature appears to contain, even at the time of writing, recurring polarised arguments that 'real' 'creativity' is related to a special talent or domain of work, and that its characteristics cannot really apply to more broad acts of everyday life [28].

The new millennium has seen increased interest in, and acceptance of, creativity's place in everyday life [29].   Sawyer[30] argues that this broadening of focus, subject areas and content, is necessary to achieve serious study of creativity.   While this differentiation and argument still recurs in literature, there is also an acceptance of the breadth of creativity described below[31].

The 1990s and after has also seen a hugely important development, in the recognition of the social context in which creativity occurs.   I will expand on this in a section below.

The focus of academic settings since the 1950s (e.g. the seminal address given by Guildford given to the American Psychological Association in 1950, and the work of Lehman in 1953) has been on the exceptional individual working in specific areas of activity, such as the arts and sciences.   Not surprisingly, the argument is that if one seeks to understand creative work, then a natural focus of attention is creative individuals and the activity commonly seen as such.

This has led to a central argument in the area of the study of creativity, that to develop the skills necessary to make original and useful changes in a domain takes not only great talent, but also a significant investment of time, believed to be 10 years[32].   This is an understandable and practical argument.   If we care about and love an area of work sufficiently to want to use it as a major form of our self-expression, the development of expertise and talent takes time and effort before we might be seen as creative within this work.   This is a practical reality, a need for time and commitment that any of us moving to a distinct form of creative expression must consider.

Yet this perspective also runs the risk that it returns us to the polarisation that this is the real creativity, and other forms of novelty, originality and usefulness are not.   Perhaps this view is what creates or supports a social stereotype of creativity that it exists in the arts and sciences, and perhaps not elsewhere[33]?

Ruth Richards [34] suggests that this intensity of focus on the exceptional or special talent means "… we let a few famous people carry the creative ball for the rest of us".   I believe we face a social and developmental challenge in recognising and accepting that 'creativity' occurs, happens and belongs in many places in our lives.

Interestingly, Richards and her co-writers, in their seminal exploration of this view of creativity, propose that 'everyday creativity' has a far larger place and impact in our lives. Pete Sanders and Arthur Bohart,[35] in a milestone development of the theories of Carl Rogers, both imply that creativity would be a natural expression of healthy personality development and an expression of self-actualisation in our lives.   Richards[36] links everyday creativity deeply into human nature in suggesting we might not be alive without a capacity to cope with, change, improvise, adapt in our environments – qualities she clearly sees as creative – and that this dynamic adjustment is a powerful way of living.   Viewed in this way she suggests everyday creativity is a way of "approaching life which can expand our experience and options ... Seen as a process ... our everyday creativity offers a whole new way of thinking, of experiencing the world and experiencing ourselves".

Richards connects this form of behaviour, "the flexible response to environmental conditions" to our genetic endowment[37]. Seen more broadly, and over time, she suggests everyday creativity also reflects our greater potential and a capacity for growth and transformation[38]. She suggests if we are more creative and focused on our growth, it reflects in "our intentions and actions". If we as individuals become healthier and more peaceful as part of our growth and development, so too will the world, she suggests[39]. These views appear, to me, to connect clearly to Rogers on the actualisation tendency and Maslow's on self-actualisation. They place our potential creativity, and its development, as a means, as Richards suggests, of "realising our higher human potential and even forwarding our on-going development"[40].

A similar view is implied and expressed in more specific theoretical terms by David Loye[41]. He connects a human tension between creativity and conformity to one of the primary evolutionary energies or pressures of our species. Loye clearly believes that the expression of creativity in whatever form might conceivably be an 'engine' of evolution in action.

Mark Runco appears to go further than Richards in his proposals[42]. He suggests "... it is human nature to be creative ... creative talents are shared among all of us, and thus creative potential is part of human nature". He makes a potentially unifying proposal amongst academics that theorise in this area: he suggests that everyday creativity is a 'domain' of activity in its own right, and thus one we can aspire to develop skills and experience in.

Runco proposes that personal creativity and its potential in any form has an underlying three-part structure: " ... discretion (deciding when to construct original interpretations and when to conform instead) and intentions (which reflect the values that motivate creative efforts) as well as the capacity to construct original interpretations of experience".

In the debate over the nature of creativity (i.e. special talent or everyday creativity), Runco proposes a practical and unifying view, suggesting that all creativity begins on a personal level, within the three factors described above, "and only sometimes becomes a social affair"[43]. He also sees the expression of creativity as a characteristic of self-actualising behaviour. He reminds us that humanistic psychologist Carl Rogers considered that creativity and self-actualisation were inextricable[44].

Whatever the location of expression that creativity may have in our individual lives, Kaufman and Baer[45] summarise a practical consideration: whether creativity can be generalised, or whether it must be domain-specific. They acknowledge that in everyday creativity it is theoretically possible to apply skills and traits in the area of creative performance in diverse domains. However, they suggest that the generality of creativity implies the work and result of "modestly creative individuals"[46]. If we divide our attention, rather than focus it in a single area of work, then our application of creativity will have different characteristics and outcomes.

Plucker and Beghetto's[47] definition arguably can embrace the polarities that occur in the academic literature: "creativity is the interplay between ability and process by which an individual or group produces an outcome or product that is both novel and useful as defined within some social context". They imply in their writing that the debate about exceptional or everyday creativity may not be important as 'creativity' can start in a small way within our everyday lives, and then may grow and develop into a different form. Overleaf I describe a potential continuum of creativity that illustrates this possibility.

My proposition, in my PhD writing, was for a continuum of creativity. Reflecting the comments described above, perhaps our creativity starts on the left-hand side of this continuum and develops if we are motivated and fortunate towards the right hand side[48]?

A 'Continuum of Creativity':

'Little-c' creativity or 'everyday' creativity.	Localised creativity or the early stages of 'intermediate-c' creativity.	'Intermediate-c' creativity	'Big-C' creativity
Characteristics: • Associated with an attitude to daily or everyday life, and its contents. Might be seen in activities like cooking or home decoration. Not necessarily acknowledged by others. • May be seen as flexibility or adaptability in approach. • Focus on an individual, or individual life. • A local domain, e.g. home or school. • The 'field' might comprise parents, friends, partners or teachers.	Characteristics: • Acts displaying newness, novelty and utility in a localised context, such as an organisation. • This creative activity will be seen and used by others, and acknowledged by them. • A localised domain, e.g. focused on the workplace or organisation. • The 'field' might comprise managers or users of the domain output.	Characteristics: • Working towards a domain-changing piece of work. • Offering a new, novel and useful potentially domain-changing piece of work that has yet to receive recognition by the 'field'. That recognition may, or may not follow. • The focus of work in the domain is likely to be beyond the local context, e.g. the domain of science or art. • The 'field' may be local, e.g. an educational institution, but with input or influence to a wider context.	Characteristics: • The new, novel, and useful process or product that changes a domain of knowledge and skill, and which receives widespread social acclaim from the relevant field. • The focus of work might be any domain of knowledge and skill. • The 'field' is likely to be broad, e.g. society, national or international in its nature.

Writers such as David Feldman[49], Mihalyi Csikszentmihalyi[50] and Anna Craft[51] propose that there is 'Big C' creativity (domain-changing work) and 'little c' creativity (which may be found in the acts of everyday life) and these are the two main types of creativity referred to. Mark Freeman[52] and Howard Gardner[53] both imply that there is a centre-ground, which Gardner calls 'intermediate creativity'. But both Gardner and Freeman use, either directly or implicitly the term 'intermediate creativity' to describe the activity of an individual who is working towards a domain-changing act of creativity and the associated recognition from the field, but has yet to achieve that status. The recognition of a middle ground, a place in which to examine 'intermediate-creativity' and its development, is a change in creativity theory seemingly only explored in the last couple of decades. I argue that the definitions of 'Big-C' and 'little-c' alone are limited and that there is a further aspect of creativity in the centre-ground that is worthy of study – i.e. investigating the novel, original and useful act of creativity that has worth and meaning in a localised context, along with the individuals who perform that work. The creativity we choose to express may be one form, and it may remain in a particular context. Yet it may also be part of a personal developmental journey, and move along the continuum described above.

In proposing the above continuum, the 'intent', focus or ambition of the creative individual may be influential in what part or stage of the continuum they may occupy and where they seek to develop. For example, if an individual doesn't seek or expect to contribute to anything other than a localised field, then they may not contribute to intermediate or 'Big C' creativity (unless they make domain changing breakthroughs unexpectedly).

The Influence of the Social Context

A further debate in the creativity literature examines whether creativity is a personal or a social phenomenon.

When I started studying creativity I held a belief described by Csikszentmihalyi[54]: that creativity originated within the person, and that it was an intra-psychic process. It is increasingly common to find researchers arguing that qualities and traits of the individual are "necessary" but not "sufficient" for the achievement of creativity[55].

Through his research Csikszentmihalyi was prompted to consider not only the "what" of creativity, but also the "where" and the "how"[56]. This involved the perspective that multiple components are present, operating as a 'system', when creativity occurs; this is often now termed a 'confluence' approach to the study of creativity. Sternberg and Lubart[57] suggest that it is the confluence perspective that allows us to take account of diverse aspects of creativity.

A systems perspective on the study of creativity has been put forward and used by Feldman, Gardner and Csikszentmihalyi (writing collectively in 1994, and individually in other sources, e.g. Csikszentmihalyi 1988, 1999; Gardner 1993 and 2006). The systems perspective moves the debate on defining creativity from "what" it is to "where" it is, or the context in which it occurs.

The perspective of the 'system' and the 'social context' suggests that the newness of a thought, act or product and its value can only be judged through social evaluation[58]. By implication, creativity is relative - the recognition and acknowledgement of creative work occur in a social environment - it is examined and recognised through the interaction between the producer of the work and the context, 'audience'[59] or 'consumer'[60]. This argument also suggests that the 'level' of creativity correlates with and is indicated by the recognition and eminence accorded by the 'field', the social context of the 'creator'[61]. According to this reasoning, creativity 'with a capital C', the kind that influences and changes a culture or context, cannot be solely in the mind and work of an individual person. It must be communicated to others in a manner they understand, which can then be assessed and accepted by them[62]. Writing at the time this theory was proposed and explored focused on 'Big C' creativity. Howard Gardner[63] at least implies the social context may be substantially more limited in some cases. Taking this further, the 'consumer' of a creative act or outcome could, conceivably, be a single person, the one responsible for the creative action.

A focus on the individual and his or her genetics is clearly not enough to explain fluctuations and differences in creativity. Advances in creativity must involve the accumulation of knowledge in a domain of skill or work, role models to indicate standards and directions, and the social communication of values, knowledge and skill[64].

The systems model proposed by Csikszentmihalyi, Gardner and Feldman has three components, the individual, the domain and the field. Csikszentmihalyi argues that creativity can be observed only at the intersection where these three components interact.

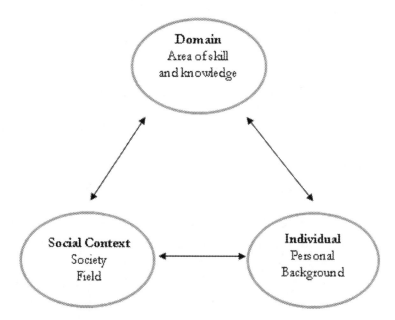

The relationships between the three parts of this model, the domain, the field and the individual, are dynamic. Each affects the others, and is affected by them. There is, therefore, no set starting point in reviewing this system. Csikszentmihalyi[65] argues that there is a spiral of influence between the domain, the person and the field, and then back to the domain in a generative cycle, as explained below. Several of my research participants told me a similar story; where they struggled as individuals with a particular subject (domain) at school, yet found a caring or inspiring teacher ('field') who supported a change in their understanding of the subject and a growth in their skill.

'Domain' of Knowledge and Skill

A domain is defined as the structure and organisation of a body of knowledge about a single topic. The domain is the area of skill or expression in which an individual would seek to be creative. The domain exists independently of the individual and has a history, language, rules and skills that can be learnt. It will involve a representational system (or "symbol system") through which the domain's knowledge will be communicated – its rules and procedures[66].

Without the existence of a domain there will be no creativity. For example, a person cannot contribute to music without access to and learning some part of the domain of music. Csikszentmihalyi argues that "creativity occurs when a person makes a change in a domain that will be transmitted through time"[67]. Access to and work within a domain is a way of earning a living for most people – but is a much stronger calling for others, particularly creative individuals[68].

The Individual

The individual is, in some way, drawn to, orientated and motivated towards a domain of knowledge and skill. Feldman[69] describes the individual as "the site of the acquisition and transformation of knowledge that has the possibility of changing domains and fields". The role of the individual is to produce some variation or change in the information or symbol system that constitutes the domain. In the context of this system, creativity occurs when the individual produces that novel change, and when it is then accepted by others, i.e. the field, and given utility and use, by its subsequent incorporation back into the structure of the domain of knowledge and skill[70].

The 'Field'

The field is defined as the social and cultural organisation of a profession, craft or job that allows or obstructs the development of work (the creation of 'products') and the recognition of creative works. The field will include individuals (e.g. parents) who mediate the access to, or influence on, the domain of individuals (e.g. children). In the early life or career of the individual, the field is likely to consist of family, relatives and/or friends that decide the acceptability of access to a particular skill, way of working or knowledge. There must usually be sufficient resources, energy and willingness from these entities, e.g. support from parents, to introduce a child to a domain, and connect the child with the field in the shape of teachers or mentors.

The field will extend to educational institutions and work places in which the individual apprentices him or herself to learn, and eventually the field may extend to include teachers, critics, opinion-makers, gatekeepers or leaders in a context, and in some cases, the general public[71]. The field will provide and even encompass the domain with "sources of support, socialisation, tradition, evaluation and recognition"[72]. The characteristics of the field will affect the rate of creativity that takes place, and the recognition it receives[73].

The Dynamics of the System

If we accept that creativity occurs 'enmeshed' in the interaction of this system, then a creative individual faces learning the content of a domain of knowledge and skill as well as the criteria and the way in which a field supports his or her work, i.e. the individual must learn and internalize the working and 'rules' of the system[74]. This framework also implies and offers an analytical structure through which creativity may be studied and / or developed [75]. Feldman[76] suggests that the three areas need to be studied individually as well as in their relationship to each other.

Csikszentmihalyi portrays the system from the perspective of 'Big C' creativity, and how the system works for large-scale and/or socially acclaimed creative acts to be recognised by and integrated into a culture. I argue that this is not the sole perspective from which the systems model can add to our understanding of the development of creativity. The social system can be used to study creativity in other contexts, specifically more localised areas.

Reflective questions:
Is 'creativity' or creative expression something you see in everyday life? In what ways?

If creativity is not something you see or believe is in everyday life, why do you think that is? Is that view or belief open to challenge or change?

What are your most natural forms of expression or skill?

Do you have a 'dream' or wish to express yourself in a particular form of skill? Is something stopping you expressing that dream? (This will be explored further in following chapters).

What activities do you remember loving as a child? Are those activities present in the same form in your life now, e.g. the skill of art, music or sport? Or are those activities reflected in a 'matured' or 'grown up' way in your adult life? If not, might they be in the future?

The chapter now turns to the description and exploration of 'Flow'.

Flow

If you listen to someone describe a deep absorption in any activity, it is common for the expression 'flow' to be used. The subjective experience relates to the development of skill and even 'happiness'. This section explores that nature of 'flow' and how this may be developed.

Summary of key points:
The subjective experience of happiness and enjoyment appears to have a recurring seven or eight part structure regardless of the work or activity undertaken and the culture in which it occurs. This subjective structure has been termed "Flow".

The component parts of 'flow' are:
Task
A challenging activity (for you) that requires skill.
Clear goals from which you can obtain immediate feedback.

Subjective state
Concentration on the task in-hand.
Merging of action and awareness.
Loss of self-consciousness.
A paradox of control.
A transformation of time.

Our attention is a precious resource. How we choose to allocate or direct our attention will influence where we might experience the 'flow' state.

The development and balancing of challenges we undertake with our skill level will grow progressively from small tasks to larger and more complex ones.

Research suggests the flow state is most commonly experienced in our 'working' world. There is a huge scope for this state to be learnt and used in our personal or privately chosen activities.

The flow state may commonly (but not always) be experienced while undertaking creative work.

One of the great gifts amongst the many challenges of undertaking PhD work is the opportunity to read a wide body of literature relating to a domain of work. This opportunity gives a student the chance to locate his or her 'heroes'; the greatest single influence on my thinking came via Mihalyi Csikszentmihalyi, from his 'Creative Vision' study with Jacob Getzels, to his work on the social system of creativity and 'flow'. I love the depth and breadth of his thinking and exploration, his readability, and I encourage you to explore his ideas and writing for yourselves. He has described 'flow' in his 1992 publication subtitled "the psychology of happiness". Nakamura and Csikszentmihalyi [77] describe flow as the subjective phenomenology of intrinsically motivated activity, activities that are rewarding in and of themselves.

Csikszentmihalyi argued, from studies that have been done over the last 3 decades (involving tens of thousands of people cross-culturally, and a wide range of different work and occupations[78]); that happiness can be cultivated and prepared for[79]. Nakamura and Csikszentmihalyi[80] are explicit: "the experience is the same across lines of culture, class, gender and age as well as across lines of activity".

'Flow' is a concept that has been used by psychologists in the examination of happiness, life satisfaction and intrinsic motivation[81]. Csikszentmihalyi proposes that individuals use broadly identical terms when they describe how it felt when they enjoyed themselves[82]. The 'phenomenology' or structure of 'enjoyment' has seven or eight primary components or parts that are remarkably similar in settings that are work-related or involve leisure. Participants in research mention at least one, if not all of them[83]. These components describe "the state in which people are so involved in an activity that nothing else seems to matter"[84], as if being "carried away by tides of a current"[85], or "flowing"[86]. The individual experiences themselves as operating at full capacity in this moment-by-moment state[87].

What are these components, or parts? I describe them below using a heading followed by other quotations, each drawn from Csikszentmihalyi's earlier writing (primarily 1992 and 1993, with a small number from his 2003 book). He has changed some of the titles, names and sequence over a decade of writing (e.g. 2003), potentially achieving a greater clarity for the reader in doing so. There is duplication in these comments, with the intention that the different words provide a 'mosaic' of descriptions of the component parts of the flow state. I will expand on how these may be used in action in chapter 2.

The experience of flow will involve an activity with clear goals and immediate feedback, with challenges balanced with available skills.

- **Clear goals and feedback**
  - The activity has "concrete goals and manageable rules".
  - "They provide clear information on how well we are doing".
  - "… concentration is usually possible because the task undertaken has clear goals and provides immediate feedback".
  - "As soon as the goals and challenges define a system of action, they in turn suggest the skills necessary to operate within it".
  - "In some creative activities, where goals are not clearly set in advance, a person must develop a strong personal sense of what he intends to do".
  - "What constitutes feedback varies considerably in different activities". Csikszetmihalyi gives a contrasting example. A surgeon may have very specific feedback when an act of surgery on a patient is 'right' or 'wrong'. A psychiatrist, in contrast may not, and have to seek subtle clues in a patient's personal state and exercise significant interpretation as to what these clues might mean.

    o   "The kind of feedback we work towards is in and of itself often unimportant … What makes this information valuable is the symbolic message it contains: that I have succeeded in my goal".

    o   "To develop skills one needs to pay attention to the results of one's actions – to monitor feedback".

Csikszentmihalyi makes clear to us that a great many activities can be the source of 'flow'. He explains that goals are likely to be many over time, and sequenced, or as I would suggest, 'nested', leading to a wide and necessary potential for skill development.

For example, to accomplish a Ph.D. there were many large components of the task, with smaller parts. To write a 'literature review' I had to read a wide body of material. Initial 'goals' were to read and understand a single academic paper. My 'feedback' was immediate: whether or not I understood the content. To someone climbing an academic 'mountain', this was a single step. A subsequent goal was to determine whether the academic paper moved on my understanding of the subject area, or not. Then I had to consider 'how' and where the information might fit within my arguments. Each was a goal, each manageable and containable in time, giving me immediate feedback as to whether I was making progress, or not. Csikszentmihalyi implies that we will see and take steps over time, increasing our skills, and allowing ourselves more complex and demanding goals.

- **"A challenging activity that requires skill**".
  - o   "A fine balance between challenges and skill".
  - o   " … challenges that require appropriate skills to realise".
  - o   "… enjoyment comes at a very specific point whenever the opportunities for action perceived by an individual are equal to (his or her) capabilities".
  - o   "Enjoyment appears at the boundary between boredom and anxiety, when the challenges are just balanced with the person's ability to act".
  - o   "It is easier to become completely involved in a task if we believe it is doable. If it appears to be beyond our capacity we tend to respond to it by feeling anxious; if the task is to easy, we become bored".
  - o   "Flow occurs when both challenges and skills are high, and equal to each other".

Csikszentmihalyi portrays diagrammatically[88] the affect of balancing challenges with skill in a task, and over time. He suggests we, or those teaching us, must balance the two in order for us to find and achieve flow, so that a challenge neither overwhelms nor underutilises our skill. For example, a high challenge with a lower level of skill may create anxiety. Low challenges, with moderate skills may yield boredom. High challenges with moderate to medium skill may take as to a state of arousal, while we learn and expand new skills. High skills with medium levels of challenge may leave us with a sense of control, but not necessarily extend us.

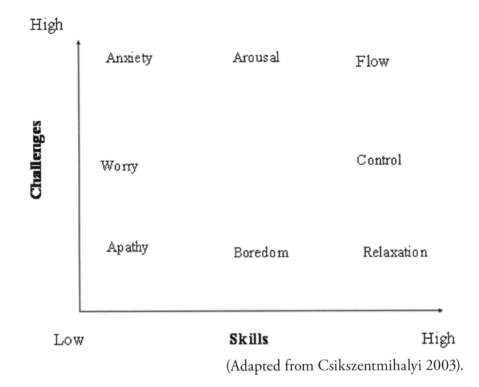

(Adapted from Csikszentmihalyi 2003).

In reading this section you might wonder why I cited the example earlier of a single academic paper as a goal relevant to achieving flow. When content is unfamiliar, when the skill to relate to content is uncertain, the reading a single academic paper is a challenge involving skill and the development of skill. Both the level of challenge and skill as perceived by the individual may relate initially to a small step or task in a small and discrete period of time. Yet the challenge and skill may build cumulatively over time.

Csikszentmihalyi[89] argues that navigating or managing this balance between challenges and skills gives us a "serviceable compass by which to find one's way through the thickets of emotional life". The path of engaging and extending skills by progressively higher challenges will, he believes, improve life quality.

The subjective state experience by the individual has some or all of the following characteristics:

- "**Concentration on the task in-hand**".
  o "Because … the challenges are high enough to absorb all of a person's skills, one needs to pay complete attention to the task at hand, and there is no attention left over to process irrelevant information".
  o "Such deep concentration … results in focusing on the present, so that problems and worries that in everyday life are a drain on psychic energy tend to disappear". "One acts with a deep (…) involvement that removes from awareness the worries and frustrations of everyday life".
  o "… enjoyable activities require a complete focusing of attention on the task in hand – thus leaving no room in the mind for irrelevant information".
  o "… the clearly structured demands of the activity impose order, and exclude the interference of disorder in consciousness".

- o "… only a very select range of information can be allowed into awareness. Therefore all the troubling thoughts that ordinarily keep passing through the mind are temporarily kept in abeyance".

An exciting consequence of balancing challenges with skill is a need for a depth of concentration and attention on a task that, by its demands, is likely to exclude other concerns, problems and worries in daily life. This form of concentration is potentially both enjoyable and relaxing.

- • "**The merging of action and awareness**".
   - o "When … skills are needed to cope with the challenges of a situation, that person's attention is completely absorbed by the activity".
   - o "There is no excess of (attention) left over to process any information but what the activity offers … people become so involved in what they are doing … they stop being aware of themselves as separate from the actions they are performing".

A further extension of the state which focuses on the present is that "events from the past or future cannot find room in consciousness". The task draws us into the present where we are "standing outside everyday routine life in a separate reality defined by the rules and demands of (the) activity"[90].

- • "**The paradox of control**".
   - o "The well-matched use of skills provides a sense of control over our actions".
   - o "If a challenges and skill are in balance, it is possible for a person to experience a sense of control".
   - o "Enjoyable experiences allow people to exercise a sense of control over their actions".
   - o "… the flow experience is typically described as involving a sense of control, or, more precisely, as lacking the sense of worry about 'losing' control that is typical in many situations of normal life".
   - o "What (is actually described) is the *possibility* rather than the actuality of control".
   - o "What people enjoy is not the sense of *being* in control, but the sense of *exercising* control in difficult situations". "Only when a doubtful outcome is at stake, and one is able to influence that outcome, can a person really know whether (he or she) is in control".

The balance of challenges and skills, concentration, action and awareness leaves those in the flow state as experiencing a sense of control. Perhaps, more importantly, it is the *possibility* of control rather than the reality of it, and a lack of worry about losing control.

- • "**The transformation of time**".
   - o " … the sense of the duration of time is altered". "Hours pass by in minutes, and minutes can stretch out to seem like hours".
   - o " … time no longer seems to pass the way it ordinarily does. The objective, external duration we measure with reference to outside events like night and day,

or the orderly progression of clocks, is rendered irrelevant by the rhythms dictated by the activity".

This suggests we lose a sense of time, or we experience a forgetting of time, time can slow *or* speed up.

- **"The loss of self-consciousness"**.
  - o "Concern for the self disappears, yet paradoxically the sense of self emerges stronger after the flow experience is over".
  - o "… there is not enough attention left over to allow a person to consider either the past or the future, or any other temporarily irrelevant stimuli".
  - o "The loss of a sense of a self separate from the world around it is sometimes accompanied by a feeling of union with the environment".
  - o "(a) loss of self-consciousness does not involve a loss of self … but rather … a loss of consciousness *of* the self. What slips below the threshold of awareness is the concept of self, the information we use to represent to ourselves who we are. … When we are not preoccupied with ourselves we actually have a chance to expand the concept of who we are. Loss of self-consciousness can lead to a self-transcendence, to a feeling that the boundaries of our being have been pushed forward".
  - o "When a person invests all (his or her) psychic energy into an interaction - whether it is with another person, a boat, a mountain, or a piece of music – (he or she) in effect becomes part of a system of action greater than what the individual self had been before. This system takes its form from the rules of the activity; its energy comes from the person's attention".
  - o "A person who pays attention to an interaction instead of worrying about the self obtains a paradoxical result. (He or she) no longer feels like a separate individual, yet her self becomes stronger. The (autoletic) individual grows beyond the limits of individuality by investing psychic energy in a system in which she is included. Because of this union of the person and the system, the self emerges at a high level of complexity".
  - o "Being less aware of oneself leaves more psychic energy to concentrate on what one is doing".

This loss of a sense of self or ego is one of the deep paradoxes of the flow state. As we focus on an activity with such concentration that there is only psychic room for the present, we may not only lose the sense of past or future concerns, we may lose the very sense of ourselves below the boundary of awareness. Yet this is *not* a negative loss. Reports argue that our actions, task and self may feel merged, as if a single 'system'. In this merging, and a growth of our skills and capacity to meet challenges within this activity, Csikszentmihalyi argues strongly that our self is actually growing, and becoming more positively complex.

Key to the concept and phenomena of flow is that it is a *subjective* state and experience influenced by the individual and environment. It is an individual's *choice* to allocate their precious resource of attention, combined with the perception of challenges and skills they have that offers the opportunity of flow in almost any activity[91]. We become primarily shaped by that which we attend to, give our attention.

I perceive two themes of urgency in Csikszentmihalyi's (1992, 1993, 2003) writings. First, again emerging from his research, he suggests the majority of those who experience 'flow' in the western world do so in the working world, rather than in private lives. It seems, he implies, many of us accept 'passive' social, relaxation and private time. Given that the flow state is associated with happiness, Csikszentmihalyi believes its structure and experience can be anticipated, taught and learnt. If we seek to develop creativity in a particular domain of activity, then surely the process of flow offers us a powerful means by which we can approach this personal development. I explore this possibility in Chapter 2.

Second, Csikszentmihalyi associates the flow state with creativity and self-actualisation, and through this believes our psychological or psychic complexity - as individuals, groups or even as a species - is increasing. He argues powerfully that this is the boundary on which we find new personal meaning. Further, he suggests that this growth and complexity represents the active edge of evolution in modern times, beyond any suggestions of changes in our physical characteristics. These are 'heady' and moving arguments in Csikszentmihalyi's writings, done in his characteristic clear writing, positive and engaging style.

It is appropriate to acknowledge that 'flow' may not be associated with creativity alone. Our relationship with a domain of activity may have different forms that may involve creativity or expertise.

For example, Policastro and Gardner[92], and Gardner writing alone[93] define four different types of relationship a person may have with a domain of knowledge and activity – what I consider possibly as 'types' of creative persons.

- A Master: is an individual who has achieved "complete mastery over one or more domains of accomplishment; his or her innovation occurs within established practice". (E.g. Mozart, Rembrandt, George Elliot.)
- A Maker: creates a new domain. E.g. Freud and psychoanalysis.
- An Introspector: is an individual concerned with "exploration of his or her inner life: daily experiences, potent needs and fears, the operation of consciousness (both that of the particular individual and that or individuals more generally)". E.g. Virginia Woolf, Annais Nin, James Joyce.
- An Influencer: "also explores the personal world, but directs his or her creative capacities towards affecting other individuals". E.g. Gandhi, Eleanor Roosevelt, Nelson Mandela.

Gardner suggests these are the "four major forms of extraordinariness" in an individual[94]. He also explains that the boundaries between these categories can overlap: e.g. Freud mastered neurology prior to 'making' psychoanalysis, and introspecting aspects of his own life - though he is remembered for his work as a "maker". The purpose in describing them is to indicate that 'creativity' is not the only way or expression through which a 'flow' state may be reached, and it may rest also in some other form of expression, such as 'expertise'.

Reflective questions:
Do you recognise experiences of 'flow'?   Where?

How did they come about?

How could you influence them recurring again?

Where would you wish to experience flow?

How might you choose a challenge in this context that balances with your skill level?   (Be ready to move in small steps, and build up from these.)

Creativity, Flow and Self-actualisation – separate and similar phenomena

Maslow writes in a manner that argues that self-actualisation involves and possibly embraces creativity. Csikszentmihalyi acknowledges 'flow' is found in the work and experiences of creative individuals.   Could these three phenomena be synonymous with each other?

Csikszentmihalyi and Maslow both write in terms that equate their respective theories with the act and experience of creativity.

Both Csikszentmihalyi and Maslow cite Ghislen[95] in his classic book on the creative process, as a source of descriptions of their respective theories[96].

Csikszentmihalyi argues strongly that "almost any description of creative experience includes experiential accounts that are in important respects analogous to those obtained from people at play" – and that the experience of 'play' is central to his examination of 'flow'[97].   Maslow equates self-actualisation and creativity and points out that boundaries between work and play become blurred[98].   When reviewing the experience of 'flow' Csikszentmihalyi was explicit that the same experiences are reported by individuals engaged in creative activities[99].

There is a clear theme running through theories associated with each of these areas acknowledging the presence and positive influence of intrinsic motivation[100].

My proposal in exploring these topics for this chapter is that self-actualisation is what we seek; creativity is one of the primary routes by which we find self-actualisation; and the flow state is the underlying structure of how this may be done.

We can enter this journey from different points on the path, and find ourselves in the experience and space of these other forms, as if one experience will take us to the others.

Concluding thoughts

I find a fascination in reading Csikszentmihalyi's work because the content and the man travels so far beyond 'psychology' alone; he draws on what one might see as philosophy and vision, and offers us a deeply moving sense of his personal 'heart'.

He suggests in his 1992 and 1993 writings that many of us find challenge and expression more in our working lives, rather than the personal; and that our free or discretionary time may be 'passively' spent. He implies that there is a sadness and a loss in that lack of balance.   He advocates that the concept and content of 'flow' gives us choice and process to bring a far greater depth of expression and experience to our personal lives.

Yet the implications and outcomes, he suggests, may go far beyond this. He suggests that the involvement in an activity we care about, and which challenges and develops us, together with the requirements for concentration and attention, bring an order and calmness to our consciousness. This sense of order may be important to us as a means of strengthening or supporting us in what can be a chaotic and changing world. As we become more involved in the experience of flow it may also become part of what contributes 'meaning' and 'purpose' to our lives. These are terms that are ambiguous and about which many people debate and write. Csikszentmihalyi implies that the 'intention' we bring to a skill and a challenge in the flow state draws us towards purpose, and is a fundamental part of what gives us 'purpose'. This may, initially, be for a physical or a sensory experience. Beyond it lies the ability to relate to and contribute to ideas and ideals.

How do we find the energy, the 'will' to start on this path? In chapter 2 I argue that emotion, or love for an activity or possibility, is central. While I may describe much of this material from what seems like a 'rational' perspective, please don't lose that connection with something we care about. At the same time I believe there is a further quality in us that is essential for reaching this intention: 'discipline'. I suspect that this may be an 'unfashionable' word to many these days, yet I ask you to look at its 'root': 'disciple'. I believe we reach outcomes and skills that matter to us by the willingness to 'follow' a path or a process that is, in its essence, disciplined or structured in a way which supports and delivers what we seek. 'Following' this path is a 'paradox', because in the 'following' it brings us to closer to an expression and a talent that is more of our true selves.

Chapter 2: How do I become Creative?

Introduction

If we recognise the potential place of creativity in our lives and personal development, the natural next question is how an individual might develop creativity, and its associated creative working practices?

This chapter is distinct from the other three in this book. I have endeavoured to base this book on an academic discipline in order to explore these core questions. However, in this chapter it is also distinctly personal. In over a decade of exploring this subject I have only found three sources, three books (which I name at the end of the chapter) that address this question in terms I have found helpful, yet that is my personal experience. It may not be yours. I believe any of us seeking to answer this question has to look for personal 'answers' that suit our lives and our style.

One of those books was 'academic'; the others were biographic, and 'self-help'. I propose to draw on and adapt the former, Keith Sawyer's 2006 work[101], and develop his suggestions on the basis of my work with students, and with coaching and psychotherapy clients.

Summary of key points:
This chapter seeks to address what I believe are two key perspectives on this subject. First, what might be your creative work? Second, ways in which you or others might develop the environment, support and skills for working in the domain. I propose to move through a natural sequence of steps or topics associated with the central question of this chapter. My intention is to prompt exploration and reflection.

I believe that the ideas I have expressed in this chapter are individual resources, a sort of 'mosaic' of possibility, rather than a 'system'. My experience argues that if you choose two or three of these to explore, your own relationship with a domain of work is likely to develop and grow. There is no 'right' idea, only something that may resonate with your own questions and aspirations.

Here are some questions that may orientate you to the thinking that follows. Explore only those that draw you or resonate for you.

Reflective questions:

- If creativity is not something you see or believe is in everyday life, why do you think that is? Is that view or belief open to challenge or change?
- What are your most natural forms of expression or skill? What activities give you most pleasure? In what activities do you experience a sense of time stopping or losing track of time?
- Do you have a 'dream' or wish to express yourself in a particular form of skill? An unlived 'dream' in the context of what you hoped your life would be? Is something stopping you expressing that dream? (This will be further explored in following chapters.)
- What activities do you remember loving as a child? Are those activities reflected in a matured or 'grown up' way in your adult life?
- As you read a summary of Howard Gardner's descriptions of multiple intelligences contained in this chapter, are there one, two or three that you immediately identify as your ways of working or expression?
- Is there one of these intelligences that you want in your life, but have not yet developed?

The Manifesto for 'Children' (or for the development of creativity)

If I were to express the key messages of this chapter in a short space, it would be through this passage: E. Paul Torrance was one of the most prolific and central researchers, writers and teachers on creativity in the last century. He wrote a short document in 1983 that he termed 'the Manifesto for Children' as a means of focusing on some behaviour that might make a crucial difference for their development.

- Don't be afraid to fall in love with something and pursue it with intensity.
- Know, understand, take pride in, practise, develop, exploit and enjoy your greatest strengths.
- Learn to free yourself from the expectations of others and to walk away from the games they impose on you.
- Find a great teacher or mentor who will help you.
- Learn the skills of interdependence.
- Don't waste time and energy on trying to be well rounded.
- Do what you love and can do well.

If I were to try and express core learning from my Ph.D. research in a very few words, I can't think of better ones than Torrance's manifesto for individuals of any age. You may wish to come back to this as a concise reminder of the journey on which you have embarked.

There is an 'essence' expressed in Torrance's remarks: 'love'. I believe your choices on creative work are likely to be characterized by that energy, as well as a vibrancy, living fully, and having a stronger sense of who you are as a person.

Do I Even Step On To This Path?

I mentioned in the introduction my friendship and fascination with an elderly artist who started me on this journey into the nature of creative lives. Her name was Catherine Yarrow. She was prolific in both her forms of art and pottery, having been a peer of artists in Paris such as Braque, Giacometti, Max Ernst, Leonora Carrington and others.

Catherine would invite young people to come and work with her, drawing and painting in her unusual garden. Commonly they would say to her 'I can't draw', messages or experiences they had encountered at school or in childhood from teachers or parents; I can't be 'creative' or do what I love, that it wasn't worth even trying.

Catherine understood that these messages had been given in the same kind of language and tone as instructions: 'you must not draw'. She would break through them with the simple statement and invitation: 'I give you permission'. It was a 'permission' to change and be different. She taught in a supportive, accepting manner.

Many of us need such 'permission' to move into creative work. Insights into what is described as 'Evolutionary Psychiatry' suggest we are genetically programmed to seek acceptance from and to get along with the 'group', our social context. To breakthrough into the 'difference' that may be associated with creativity we may need that permission to try, learn and express a 'difference' from others.

For many the experience may include aspects of fear and inner resistance to change. In the following passages I will include comments on how these feelings may be encountered and become part of the creative work itself.

Stepping on to the 'path' may also be a reflection of a time in your life when new choices need to be made, and earlier choices made and not made need to be revisited. This experience, too, will be part of the writing that follows.

In taking this step, making a choice that is personal and will involve effort, give some thought as to 'why' you are doing this. In the writing that follows I will prompt you to reconsider and develop these ideas.

How Do I Find 'My' Creativity?

This is the question that drew me, as an individual, to this field of study. Students and clients I work with also commonly ask it.

Csikszentmihalyi, writing on 'flow', argues that the state can be found in almost any activity. Keith Sawyer[102] cites Csikszentmihalyi and Amabile as considering flow and creativity to be synonymous. Therefore, the blunt or immediate answer to this question might be that creativity could be found in almost any activity. The main need may be for us to choose one, and experiment, play or have a go.

I believe there are different ways of finding a more personal answer. You may wish to take time with and reflect on any of the following sections. Naomi Wolf[103] has strong words for this step:

> "…draw everything to a complete stop until you can listen deeply to your soul, identify your heart's desire, and change direction." (p4). "… go somewhere quiet and listen inwardly. What you hear internally might completely surprise you; and it won't be true unless you hear it first internally."

These may be strange or strong words, yet I believe that 'love' or 'passion' for an activity may be central to what follows.

What do you love doing?

A natural and human place to start this search is by asking "what do you love doing?" What is the place of human activity that you love to be? Where (drawing on the 'flow' concept) do you find 'time stops'? This will, hopefully, give you the primary indication of where you most wish or need to be.

Yet it doesn't always. Let me give you an example. I once interviewed a psychotherapist as part of a piece of research. He was and is a strongly talented creative man independently of his occupation as a psychotherapist. As part of the natural focus of his professional work he believed he should work on the 'illness' or 'pathology' that troubled his clients – he decided he should make a specialism of 'depression'. I asked him, during our interview, 'Why aren't you working on helping your clients find their creative work, the activities they love?', as this appeared to have such a strong connection to the rest of his being and life experience. He didn't answer; he appeared to ignore me completely. A few minutes later I asked the same question, and again he appeared to ignore me completely. I let the matter go, and finished the interview. As I was packing my papers to leave, I said, 'I just have to ask you – why did you ignore my question about why aren't you working on helping your clients find their creative work, the activities they love?' He started at me, speechless. He hadn't even heard my question. The idea that he might choose a specialism that he was uniquely prepared to explore and support was one he was 'deaf' to – he was going down a professional path that he believed his profession demanded of him, the cure of 'illness' rather than the support of the creative strength and expression of the human heart. I believe many of us may focus on what we think others or our profession expects us to do, rather than ask the more important question of what we would love to do. We may not even 'hear' the question or call to a creative work that we may love.

The majority of people I work with also stare at me blankly when I ask them what they love to do. If there is not an 'obvious' answer to this question, there are more indirect places in which an answer might be found.

What did you love doing as a child?

When I interviewed 40 middle-aged individuals with a reputation for creativity as part of my PhD research there was a core theme that emerged. Whether the individual had found and developed their creative work early in life, or later, they were <u>all</u> focusing on an activity they had found and enjoyed in their childhood. Therefore, if you feel you have not yet found or associated with a creative activity or domain of work, a key starting point is the question of what you loved doing as a child.

Exploring this possibility might offer a 'literal' or 'symbolic' answer to the 'form' of creative work.

For example, one individual I met in my research had become a scientist after being shown the excitement that could exist in the subject by a talented and caring teacher, and that he, the student, could do something he did not believe himself capable of. This example illustrates the 'literal' answer and a concept described as 'the crystallizing experience' by Walters and Gardner[104]: "... such experiences involve remarkable and memorable contact between a person with unusual talent and potential and the materials of the field in which that talent will be manifested…their dramatic nature focuses the attention of the individual on a specific material, experience or problem".

Another individual told me how he loved going on imaginary journeys as a child, and how he would 'colour pictures' of those journeys. Travel and growth on journeys became central to his life, as did filming his travels. I believe my own fascination with individual stories as a child reflects in the work I now undertake. These possibilities illustrate a 'symbolic' answer found in earlier childhood experience. Pleasure found as a child may be transformed into an adult activity of a related form.

The point in these examples, which I have explored with others, is that our love and fascination with an activity as a child stands a very strong chance of being the literal or symbolic activity that would be pleasurable and vital to us as an adult. I ask those I work with, as a routine: 'what did you love doing as a child?' and explore what opportunities that experience offers now, to the individual as an adult.

Implied in these descriptions is the possibility that there may be some activity that we loved that we have forgotten, or chosen not to follow that we can turn to now, at a different part of our lives. Your creative activity and choice may be an experience or 'seed' from long ago you are called to return to, to develop in a way that corresponds to your age now.

What forms of 'intelligence' are most naturally yours?

If the questions so far do not yield a clue to the individual, I use the framework, developed by Professor Howard Gardner, of 'multiple intelligences'.

Howard Gardner is a Professor of Psychology at Harvard University. He has worked extensively and experimentally in areas like cognitive psychology. Well over 20 years ago he started to take the view that intelligence is not a unitary concept – as most researchers had tended to believe. Brain scans of individuals using 'traditional' mental problem-solving-type intelligence show one part of the brain only being activated. Not unreasonably, Gardner asked what the rest of the brain was for! He also realised that when other parts of an individual's skill were used different parts of the brain became activated. He proposed seven, and then subsequently ten, different forms of intelligence.

To recognize talent and a gift, one has to have a descriptive language for them. My experience is that most people do not have such a language or even recognize such a need. Many of us 'project' creativity onto classical areas such as music and art and on to 'other people out there'. Generally, 'intelligence' in a subject area can become ability, expertise and a talent as the precursor to 'creativity'. I.e. one has to learn a skill in order to relax comfortably in that skill and be creative and adaptable with it. Gardner, by giving us ten areas of possible attention and language, has allowed us to acknowledge that expertise and creativity can occur in any of these places! What follows are summary descriptions of his ten 'intelligences' drawn from his book 'Intelligence Reframed' [105].

- Linguistic Intelligence
  - A sensitivity to spoken and written language.
  - The skill of using and learning language.
  - Example jobs include writers and poets, speakers, actors and lawyers.

- Logical-mathematical Intelligence
    - The capacity and skill to logically analyse problems and relationships.
    - This may be seen in mathematics and the sciences.
    - Example jobs include scientists and mathematicians.

- Musical Intelligence
    - The sensitivity to the pitch and rhythm of musical patterns.
    - The skills of appreciating, composing and/or performing music.
    - Gardner views musical intelligence as closely paralleling linguistic intelligence.

- Bodily-kinaesthetic Intelligence
    - The use of the whole body, or parts such as the hands or mouth, to communicate, act, perform or fashion products and outcomes.
    - Example jobs include dancers, actors, athletes, as well as crafts-people such as surgeon's and mechanics who focus on talent expressed with their hands.

- Spatial Intelligence
    - The capacity and skill to perceive and transform patterns in wide space or confined areas.
    - Example jobs include pilots and navigators, as well as sculptors, surgeons, graphic artists and architects.

- Interpersonal Intelligence
    - The sensitivity, skill and capacity to understand the motivations, intentions and desires or others, and consequently to work with and influence others.
    - Example jobs include salespeople, teachers, religious leaders, politicians and actors.

- Intra-personal Intelligence
    - The capacity to understand and have an effective relationship with oneself, along with having a concept or working model of oneself, such as fears and desires. To use this information in developing one's life.
    - Example jobs include writers, psychologists and psychotherapists.

- Naturalist Intelligence
    - This involves a capacity and an expertise to recognise and classify the species of flora and fauna on one's environment.

- Spiritual Intelligence
    - Gardner appears less clear in discussing and defining this intelligence.
    - It reflects the motivation, desire and capacity to know about experiences and perceived cosmic entities that make sense of life beyond ourselves, or in relationship to our wider world.
    - Gardner acknowledges that this may involve many different forms of spiritual experience.

- Existential Intelligence
  - Gardner acknowledges that this might be a sub-set of spiritual intelligence.
  - This involves the capacity to orientate and locate oneself in relation to the existential experience of human life, such as the meaning of life and death, the development of physical and psychological worlds, and profound experiences like the love of another person, or immersion in the experience of art or a work of art.

What does this mean in practical terms for us as individuals, or parents of growing children expressing these possibilities? Gardner suggests we have all of these intelligences. However, my experience suggests that we are born predisposed or sensitized to show two or three quite strongly. Unusually a child can show some capacity very early on, say a few months old. My personal interpretation is a more 'normal' route is that you will see signs of these intelligences showing sometime from 6 years old plus. In my work with students and clients I ask them to consider two or three of the 'intelligences' they are particularly 'at home' or sensitized in. This information, again, becomes a clue or a pointer to areas of activity in which you may find a choice of creative activity, either in the individual 'intelligences', or in how they might combine and relate. The range and type of these intelligences also communicate a further important message: creativity may be found in so many different forms of expression, both 'product' and 'process'.

What 'domain' do you wish to work in?

Whether we have a direct answer to an area of activity we love and feel comfortable working in, or a speculative one as a result of identifying which of these intelligences we relate to, we are, in practical terms, seeking a 'domain' of skill and activity to develop and explore.

Stages or steps beyond this point in the chapter assume that you have made a choice of activity in which to seek expression and experience.

What Support For Your Aspirations Exists In The 'Field'?

Reminding you, the 'field' is the social context, the social 'soil' in which you will seek to develop and grow this activity. Make your choices carefully, and be willing to change them in support of yourself.

Where do you wish to learn and work with this activity? Look around. Get to know what is available. Talk to people. Don't assume a single location is all there is, or accept the experience of one location as defining all possibilities. Ask yourself: does this context readily accept newcomers? Is there support for exploration and learning? Is there an availability of teachers and mentors? Does this teaching occur in a style that matches how you learn? Is the environment respectful and accepting? Has this context the capacity to match challenges of activity to your developing skill? Look for the place where you can learn and discover.[106]

Be willing to change 'field' if your needs aren't met, if you are unsupported. Many of us to readily accept social messages from those in a 'field' that we have not the ability to learn an activity. Experience tells me that the reality is very different, that the issue is more likely to be associated with the capacity of the 'field' to teach or support us.

Your priorities and needs will change as your skill develops. For example, at the outset you may need some explicit teaching. However, as your skill develops, the need may become that of mentoring, someone who will give you the freedom to explore and grow as you wish and feel best.

Look For A Mentor

It is a consistently reported aspect of the development of creativity that individuals have a 'mentor'. This matter is explored in substantial detail in the next chapter. A mentor is someone who may teach and nurture us as we learn. Stories of creative lives argue that the mentor has a catalyzing effect on our potential development, passing on talent across a generation, providing a relational 'mirror' through which we learn more about ourselves through the responses and support of a more experienced individual. Csikszentmihalyi has a wonderful expression; that we 'metabolize' the attention of the mentor, providing a fuel for our growth and efforts.

Key here is the role of a mentor to provide a supportive, safe, accepting environment in which skills may be developed.

One of the suggestions I make in chapter 3 is we are moving into a time where individuals 'self-mentor'. By this I mean that we might identify our exemplars or heroes in work, and emulate their practices, even if we do not have direct contact with them. This could be done via 'distance' means, such as reading, TV programmes, or study.

Challenge Or Expand Your Normal Way Of Working?

Our 'normal' ways of working will shape how we move into a new domain of activity. Yet if 'creativity' is about new, unusual and useful insights, perhaps those qualities need also to be brought to our ways of working.

If one of your characteristic ways of working might cause you a difficulty, consider an alternative. For example, don't be isolated or introverted. Talk to others about your work; share your enthusiasm and interest.

Motivate Yourself 'Intrinsically'

Creativity research is very specific: the strongest outcomes are likely to be found in individuals that are 'intrinsically' motivated, that is motivated from within, rather than externally. Make choices from what motivates *you*. Working solely to the wishes, standards or ideas of others doesn't necessarily help and may conceivably hinder your goals. Personal energy and motivation are more likely to be there via what *we* care about. Creative individuals I have known or read about work for the joy and relationship with their activity, not fame or income. Yet we are in a society that seems to imply that a path such as this is not 'validated' or appropriate unless it achieves recognition, if not 'fame'. It may take effort to respect our own choice and authority and not be overwhelmed by society's voices and pressures that suggest we should do something else.

Use the Working Habits of Creative Individuals

If we look at the lives of individuals who have a relationship with creativity, their patterns of work are remarkably consistent.

The time it takes to learn:

My own experience suggests that a priority for individuals entering creative work is a sense of 'reality' about the time it takes to learn a way of working. It is almost a cliché these days to say we are in a fast-changing world. I believe we are surrounded by messages and stereotypes that suggest most things can be done quickly, that we could and should be able to learn skills rapidly and be good at something without much effort or practice. The stories of creative individuals suggest that reality is different. Acquiring a skill or expertise takes time; depending on our aspirations a considerable time may be needed. The skill we gain will be in service of both the discipline we are working in, and emotions or feelings we seek to express through it[107].

Being willing to keep working, to accept 'good' and 'bad' outcomes:

Many of us would wish or expect to do 'good' work all the time, and get dispirited if that is not the case. Yet for every good piece of work we do, the chances are that there will be equal or greater numbers of lesser quality. The willingness to work and produce the 'good' and the 'bad' is the process of practice and refining skill, 'trial and error'. The repetition of work is a means of exploration. This way of working allows us to refine skill, and offers us the chance to combine different parts or forms of our work in different ways. This willingness is also what raises the probability of good work being produced. The willingness to work, and accept outcomes of different quality are central to creative work. Skills take time to learn. Successes and errors are likely to occur in the same periods of time, because our 'mistakes' are also part of our skill development and practice. To experience discomfort and degrees of 'mess' as part of these work processes is quite normal. An ex-boss of mine used to say: "if you are not making mistakes, you are not trying". This was his way of saying you are unlikely to be pushing the use of your skill to an 'edge' unless you also accept the risk of mistakes.

Reflective time and practice is a constructive way of working with these experience. If we can approach work believing there is no right or wrong, only exploration and steps forward we may free our energy to work.

Patterns of productivity:

'Productivity' is more important than accuracy or being right. Creative individuals tend to be 'productive'. More attention is paid to working and producing. It is as if the act of working, exploring, gaining experience means that both 'good' and 'bad' pieces of work might be produced at the same time. Be willing to make errors. Work on more than one thing, multi-task. Take time off, relax, distract yourself from the work, and find that ideas will still come as you do so. Creative individuals tend to say 'work is play'.

Being a 'perfectionist' is potentially a form of tyranny likely to obscure or obstruct our work. Life's quality and work are mixed. It is an illusion if we believe that we can consistently achieve 'perfection'.

Having chosen something that is important to you and your self-expression, work hard. Be willing to take time to learn. Develop patience and accept ambiguity. If I use my Ph.D. research as an example, its essence was a creative question – how does creativity change as individuals age. I had my question, but I didn't know the 'answer' or even the route to an answer at the outset. The implication was that I spent time learning what was needed, and living with considerable amounts of fear and anxiety while I *didn't know* what the 'answer' or route to the answer might be. Even now, in sitting down to write this material, I am again dealing with ambiguity as I reshape previously written material, and write new passages. In all of this I have to learn all over again to clarify my 'question' and have the patience and tolerance of ambiguity will I find an 'answer'. I believe this is a core creative skill.

Dealing with inner 'resistance' to creative work:

Many individuals associated with creative work will tell you of the experience of inner resistance, a feeling or wishing to be somewhere else, or to avoid even starting creative activity. Resistance is a state I know well! I believe it is likely to be more 'normal' than unusual. Some creative individuals I know live in very clean houses, because their way of avoidance and resistance is to clean the house before they start their creative work!

I believe we have individually to find our own answers to dealing with inner resistance. I use one that comes from Cameron (1992) – writing a journal for a defined time each day, to write about and explore my resistance *before* I sit down and work. It is if I say: "okay, resistance is not to be resisted; let me sit down and 'write it out' before I drop it, and do the work I set out to do." Writing a journal allows me to explore my uncertainty or fear about a piece of work, to know it, and then calms me before I move into doing the work itself. Many of us find an experience implied in Bohart (2007): we have what feels like different 'voices' within us, and the voice of 'resistance' to creative work may carry some message or concern that needs to be dealt with in a practical way.

These concerns may reflect a fear of failure. Drawing on what I have written above, 'failure' represents an experiment, an attempt which may bring information or feedback to coach us forward into a new attempt.

Trust the process to contain and shape your activity:

I have a strong belief in the 'process', the way of working leading us to outcomes that we seek and value. Even when I am self-doubting and unsure about my ability to achieve a piece of work, I will trust the process of undertaking a piece of work to move me to an outcome. I bring myself to the table, sit down and work. For example, the process of writing about 'flow' for these chapters has involved months of reading in order to explore what I could actually 'say'. I have been in a state of uncertainty and tension for much of that time, yet I have trusted the process of working, to lead to an understanding and a written outcome.

Developing or Entering the 'Flow' State

Csikszentmihalyi has explained that 'happiness' has recurring components. From many of his examples, 'happiness' is associated with an expression and performance of skill. If this could be 'taught' or 'learnt, we have a means of affecting our own life quality and state.

We can raise the possibility and frequency of 'flow' experiences by seeking work or parts of work that balance our challenges with our skills.

What follows is an interpretation of how this may occur. There is some repetition here from chapter 1. I have reduced the number of components of 'flow' to those that I believe most affect the 'starting out' into an area of skill and expression.

- <u>A challenging activity that requires skill</u>

I believe the task of finding the balance between 'challenges' and 'skill' to be the primary place in which the flow state is located, and through which the other factors occur. Csikszentmihalyi[108] argues that navigating or managing the balance between challenges and skills gives us a "serviceable compass by which to find one's way through the thickets of emotional life". The path of engaging and extending skills by progressively higher challenges will, he believes, improve life quality. Csikszentmihalyi portrays diagrammatically [109] the affect of balancing challenges with skill in a task, and over time. *He suggests we, or those teaching us, must balance the two in order to find and achieve flow.* The diagram below is an adaptation of several shown in Csikszentmihalyi's 2003 work.

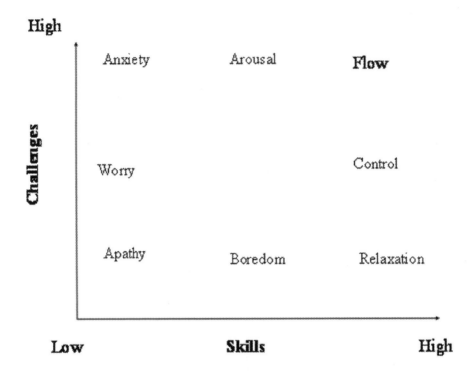

To enter the flow state we are consistently managing this balance over time. The same balancing task faces us, whether we are just starting out in learning an area of work, or demonstrating more established skill. This task involves identifying the size of task my skills can undertake at this stage in my knowledge and development. If I am new to an area of work, then the choice I need to make will be small. The task may involve a piece of work lasting only a few minutes. Csikszentmihalyi suggests to us we should, ideally, push ourselves to the edge of our skills; pick a challenge that is on the edge of what we can cope with. If we 'fail', we may need to reduce the size of step we take, and try again. In this way we are navigating the relationship between our skills and the challenges we face. Csikszentmihalyi explains that enjoyment occurs when this balance is found, where the opportunities for action equal our skill.

Reminding ourselves (from his 1992, 1993 and 2003 writing) of how Csikszentmihalyi describes this element:

• **Clear goals and feedback**.

In order to balance challenges with our skill we need clear goals and feedback from the task at hand. The goals, and feedback, will support our capacity to concentrate. A goal is what I am setting out to do. What represents feedback will vary with the characteristics of a task. Csikszentmihalyi gives two contrasting medical examples. A surgeon working on a patient will have very clear boundaries for what is 'right' and 'wrong'. A psychiatrist, in contrast, may only see subtle clues about a patient's state and may have to exercise interpretation as to what these clues mean. Put simply, the feedback we seek tells is whether or not we have reached our goal.

Csikszentmihalyi explains that goals are likely to be many over time, and sequenced or as I would suggest, 'nested', one inside a bigger one, leading to a wide and necessary potential for skill development. Smaller goals cluster together to become bigger goals overall.

To balance challenges with skill, while working towards a goal through feedback, supports one of our most valuable resources: a capacity to focus our attention and concentrate.

- "**Concentration on the task in-hand**".

Our ability to concentrate may not be immediate or come easily. Like so many things, it may take practice. For example, can we hold our attention on a task for 15 or 30 minutes? Can we develop our ability to do this consistently over time via practice? Potentially the size of our goal may need to be limited to a small number of minutes to allow this skill of concentration to develop. Our capacity to concentrate eventually becomes a gift. The need for a depth of concentration and attention on a task is likely to exclude other concerns, problems and worries in daily life. This form of concentration is potentially both enjoyable and relaxing. This becomes another argument for why it is worth working to develop.

A further consequence of this concentration is that we become absorbed, that action and awareness feel as if they have become one.

- "**The merging of action and awareness**".

A further extension of the gift of concentration, the state which focuses on the present is that "events from the past or future cannot find room in consciousness". The task draws us into the present where we are "standing outside everyday routine life in a separate reality defined by the rules and demands of (the) activity"[110].

My interpretation is that the development, the practice of these behaviours and ways of being become the gateway, the doorway into entering the flow state.

Reflective questions and guidance on 'Flow': [111]
Can you choose a task or activity that would be challenging to your present level of skill?

Choose a task that you can complete in the time available to you. This may mean choosing a small 'piece' of work from which to develop.

What goal is this task serving /seeking? What feedback does performance of this task offer you? How do you know how well or otherwise you are performing? What are the 'rules' you are following?

Focus on the task. Let the task absorb your attention. Practise your concentration; if you find it wavers to begin with, keep practising.

How can you relax as you complete this task, let go of 'worry' that you might lose control?

Gradually increase the complexity of the task you undertake as your skill increases.

Concluding thoughts

Restating what I explained at the beginning of this chapter: I believe that the ideas I have expressed are individual resources, a sort of 'mosaic' of possibility, rather than a 'system'. My experience argues that if you choose a small number of these to explore (as little as two or three) your own relationship with a domain of work is likely to develop and grow. There is no 'right' idea, only something that may resonate with your own questions and aspirations.

Making a choice to attempt a particular form or process of creative work as important to you, being willing to develop the necessary competence and to do so in relationship to supportive individuals, such as mentors), is seen as a means of asserting 'self-determination'. The ideas contained in the Chapter 1 discussion on self-actualisation also suggest it may involve many of the psychological characteristics of 'happiness' [112].

Supportive books for this exploration:

In the introduction to this chapter I mentioned three books that described these steps in a detail and quality that I had not seen elsewhere.

Cameron, J. (1992) The Artist's Way. London: Pan Books.

Sawyer, R.K. (2006). Explaining Creativity: The Science of Human Innovation. Oxford: Oxford University Press.

Wolf, N. (2006). The Tree House. London: Virago Press

Keith Sawyer has written a book fundamentally academic in its approach. The book is in plain language, and explores creativity from many perspectives and domains of work, together with providing ideas for action at its end.

Julia Cameron and Naomi Wolf are 'teachers' who have taught 'creativity' in different forms for many years. Julia Cameron's book is a structured 'course' in creativity with clear steps, views, guidance, and 'tools'. Naomi Wolf has written a beautiful biographic exploration of time spent with her father and how he taught and inspired creativity in students over his life time. Both use a beautiful language likely to inspire and support changes of this nature.

In the passages of this chapter I have described the influences of a 'mentor'. The next chapter moves to explore the nature, content, actions and contribution of mentoring. One of my primary goals in writing this book is that it might act as a form of mentoring at a distance to readers.

Chapter 3: What Is The Contribution Of Mentoring?

"They needed me to be curious about them and to love them; they needed me to help them imagine themselves." (Wolf 2006: p89).

Introduction

The role of the mentor and the contribution of mentoring emerged as the biggest single surprise to me in my PhD research. Wherever you look in stories or literature on creativity, you may expect to find a 'mentor'.

What surprised me further from my research participants was that the stronger an individual's reputation for creative work, the more 'mentors' or influential adults they would describe. This contribution from other people didn't appear to be confined to younger years. When someone changed work content or process they would turn to others for ideas and inspiration. Mentoring didn't just 'happen', individuals searched out or opened to sources of help, either close at hand, or at a distance.

Mentoring as a concept and an action has its roots in myth (the Odyssey) two and a half thousand years ago, and frequent patterns of use through to modern times Yet it might also be viewed as clichéd as a concept or a practice, and with the best of some of its possibilities overlooked in a search for a more modern and glossy 'development' tool or activity.

My argument in this chapter is that mentoring has never been more central to achieving individual development and performance potential than it is now. The concept of 'scaffolding' exists in developmental psychology as a core basis of child development (e.g. Oates 1994). The older person provides a support and a lead to the younger. The action and response of the older person becomes a 'relational mirror' through which the younger person learns more of themselves, their world and their ability. My PhD research into developmental patterns of individuals acknowledged for their creativity implies that this 'scaffolding' and 'relational mirror' persists in key milestones from childhood into and through adult life. The creative individual will not only be mentored early in life, but throughout life. They will be distinguished by the number of individuals that influence them and by how they eventually search out people to shape their understanding, development and performance. They move into acts of what I have come to describe as self-mentoring, taking ownership and responsibility for their own growth.

Reports of mentoring in the arena of science[113] communicate its capacity for inter-generational development; it becomes the means by which one generation supports the creation of work in the next generation. Further, that individuals in receipt of mentoring of this quality will pass this gift of attention on to others, extending its influence.

There is an extensive body of research cited within this chapter that communicates a wealth of details of mentoring at different times of life and types of working discipline. New research (Keinanen and Gardner 2004) coming from a social systems perspective of creativity and mentoring (e.g. Csikszentmihalyi 1999) suggests that the form mentoring may take will be influenced by the type of work an individual seeks to learn. For some it is a very structured and directed 'teaching' of a skill. For others it is a form of inspiration and uncovering of their personal talents and motivation.

This chapter:
- Communicates the contribution, gift and power of mentoring, motivating others to explore this role.
- Reviews literature on mentors and mentoring associated with the childhood and adulthood of gifted and creative individuals.
- Summarises core actions, experiences and environments associated with mentoring.
- Argues that the essence of mentoring is not only 'actions' but values and intentions to sponsor the growth of another person.
- Proposes that a theme identified in the work of Keinanen and Gardner (2004) on horizontal mentoring reflects a pattern of 'self-mentoring' identified in Worth (2000) and Zuckerman (1977).

Seen together, I believe these contributions offer a more complete picture of what mentoring may do and can accomplish. There is a perspective, for example, that parents cannot 'mentor', and that early-life support is different from what may follow. I do not share either of those views, and will seek to make that case, particularly where there are increasing grounds to believe there are many different mentorial roles in life [114]. I consider the act of mentoring one of the most powerful contributions we have in preparing a younger generation to respond to the challenges of the difficult times in which we live.

Summary of key points:
Research on creative lives argues the influences that create an atmosphere and experience of mentoring in the early years were:
- *The home environment: homes as places where there was a love of learning.*
- *Homes were where children were stimulated and encouraged into exploring and learning activities.*
- *Areas within the home were set aside for the child's work, practice and development, and they were commonly excused from finding work outside the home.*
- *The focus, actions and behaviours of parents: parents were child-focused, or child-centred, devoting both time and energy to the needs of the talented child.*
- *Parents modelled a strong work ethic, a productive use of time, the setting of high standards, and an interest in creative activities, e.g. arts and sciences.*

- *These young people were commonly given the freedom to explore and find their own interests and parents placed strong emphasis on building and developing the child's chosen interest.*
- *Parents located and organised teachers for the talented child when their interest became clear.*
- *The teachers were of progressively higher skills, to match the child's development, and combined with the parents, made the process of learning enjoyable, challenging and safe.*
- *The impact of schooling and teachers: The positive effects of schooling are consistently found in the contact with a certain type of teacher or mentor.*
  - o *The teacher who proves a major influence on development will have a more direct, personal approach to teaching.*
  - o *These teachers often 'role modelled' a level of interest in a subject that may otherwise appear without purpose, or as boring, and did so in a way which proved inspiring to the younger person.*
  - o *They engaged children actively by their teaching style, and were respectful of the results achieved by them.*
  - o *The challenges provided by the teachers were carefully paced with the skill level already achieved by the young person.*
  - o *The influential teacher demonstrated an individual concern and caring for the young person, providing additional activities which allowed a development of skill.*
  - o *A common theme that ran through this work is that the teachers "recognised" a talent in the young person, and, with these other factors, drew out that ability.*

*Mihalyi Csikszentmihalyi describes the underlying process graphically: "**talented children can grow into talented adults only by metabolising the attention of parents, teachers, coaches, mentors ....**"*

In adulthood the role and influences are summarised as:
- *This would be someone who would offer unconditional support (affective) and an understanding (cognitive) that explored and gave feedback on the nature of their work.*
- *Mentors might perform a range of different roles:*
  - o *Paragons ("those whom the artist admired, imitated, emulated, copied, idolised or was otherwise influenced by") and associates ("acquaintances, contacts, fellow members of movements or societies but who could not be considered rivals, collaborators, co-pupils, friends or siblings") emerged as the most influential on the eminence of the artist*
  - o *A teacher who enhanced skills and intellectual development.*
  - o *A sponsor to facilitate entry.*
  - o *A host and guide who welcomed the newcomer to their area of work.*
  - o *An exemplar, for the rules and achievements of a domain of work.*
  - o *A counsellor for moral support at times of stress.*
  - o *A protector of a younger person as they ventured into the uncertainties of a new area of work.*
- *Mentors 'modelled' many different values, skills and working styles, such as:*
  - o *The thrill of scientific enquiry.*
  - o *The pleasure of working with particular materials.*
  - o *Creative and quality thinking.*
  - o *Integrity and honesty in work.*

- o *Openness to openness – a free flow of information, openness to experience and receptiveness to the unexpected.*
- o *A capacity to form and work to 'dreams' – integrating both ideas and scientific disciplines of work.*
- o *Responsibility – to society, the domain of knowledge, others and oneself.*

What Is A 'Mentor'?

At its simplest the dictionary describes the mentor as a "wise or trusted guide". There are individuals seen, in the classic sense, as a mentor. In stories, they are the teacher, the boss, the older colleague. The role described and implied by Daniel Levinson and his colleagues[115] includes:

- A teacher of skills.
- A 'sponsor' or 'guide' into a new working environment.
- An 'exemplar' of skills, achievements, ways of working.
- A coach or counsellor.
- Someone who will 'believe' in and see the qualities of the younger person as they 'find' themselves.

My argument and experience from PhD research is that, while this definition is sound and holds, the 'mentor' can and should be seen more broadly. When seen as someone who 'scaffolds' the development of another, and provides a relational mirror through which they learn, then this role recurs at key predictable points in the lifespan.

Levinson, in his later work[116], makes an important distinction. He writes: "mentoring cannot be understood in purely individual terms as the activity of a single person. It is a relationship which the two participants conjointly initiate, form, sustain, exploit, benefit and suffer from, and, ultimately, terminate. The nouns 'mentor' and 'mentee' identify the participants. But the verb 'to mentor' is essential in identifying the drama they are engaged in. The essence of the drama is the evolution of the mentoring relationship." John-Steiner[117] argues that many relationships can be mentorial in nature, and cites family, lovers, teachers and peers each having a slightly different contribution. She goes further in acknowledging the influences of those at a distance of geography or time, such as artists and authors. These ideas suggest that mentoring can be direct, in terms of a relationship with another person, or indirect through influence attributed to another person who may be 'known' via another medium.

Reviewing The Contribution Of Mentoring And Influential Adults Over The Lifespan.

Mentoring in the early years

Literature and research on the patterns and mentoring in lives of creative, gifted and eminent individuals has been remarkably consistent over time in their reports. These themes also show in more recent research and that which would be described as 'normal' development'.

Studies of the development of creative and eminent individuals, and those of the development of talented teenagers suggest that the home background provides focused and detailed support during the young person's development. John-Steiner[118] suggests that in the past parents might have commonly taught gifted children themselves. Parents today may have to "create settings and opportunities which affect the individual development of the child."

These homes were commonly places where there was a love of learning and space allowed for support of it[119], where children were stimulated and encouraged into exploring and learning activities[120]. Studies cited below offer practical descriptions and specific details.

Bloom[121], in a widely quoted study of 125 individuals who achieved eminence across 6 domains of skill, described in some detail the actions of such parents in encouraging and nurturing growth in their children.

- Parents were child-focused, or child-centred, devoting both time and energy to the needs of the talented child.
- They modelled a strong work ethic, a productive use of time, the setting of high standards, and an interest in creative activities, e.g. arts and sciences.
- They located and organised teachers for the talented child when their interest became clear. The teachers were of progressively higher skills, to match the child's development, and combined with the parents, made the process of learning enjoyable, challenging and safe.
- Areas within the home were set aside for the child's work, practice and development - and they were commonly excused from finding work outside the home.

These young people were commonly given the freedom to explore and find their own interests[122] and parents placed strong emphasis on building and developing the child's chosen interest[123]. These findings are echoed by more recent work. John-Steiner[124] illustrates that parental habits such as reading, love of literature and open-minded exploration of the surrounding world can become values or a model of behaviour used by a child in a chosen domain of interest. Further, that "the home atmosphere supported the adventurous spirit of those young people who were considering a creative career. It was the parent's enthusiasm rather than specific instruction in art and science that helped their development". In the absence of a network of support and encouragement the young people commonly reported lower qualities of experience and performance in their skill development[125]. Where the parental focus was on academic grades, rather than learning, the young person reported perceptions of pressure rather than encouragement. In a home of a lower social class parental influence and encouragement was seen as particularly necessary to support the child's development against a poor or socially marginal background[126].

Goertzel and Goertzel[127] highlight for us that the home experiences may be difficult for many creative and eminent individuals. These experiences often became part of the type of creativity produced, e.g. in actors and writers drawing on the conflicts found in their home. The experience and witnessing of this environment, and often parental failure, they suggest may free the creative individual from fears of failure they might otherwise have developed[128].

Both historical studies of eminent individuals and more recent studies of the development of talented children illustrate a common and significant disaffection in their experience of school and the classroom[129]. A range of problems are mentioned: boring curriculum, dull or cruel teachers, bullying; a significant estrangement between creative pupils and their teachers; a wish by the teenagers not to be doing what they were doing; there being no perceived effect of school, even high school, on the individuals; and that teachers personally and occupationally face practical difficulties in altering these circumstances. A number of authors[130] imply or speculate directly that schooling appears to seek to level-down students to a common group, that the performances they seek and accept are limited - and in the act of doing this they threaten or limit the developmental opportunities and potentials of talented and gifted individuals.

The positive effects of schooling are consistently found in the contact with a certain type of teacher or mentor. The teacher who proves a major influence on development will move beyond an institutional 'role', and into a more direct, personal approach to teaching[131]. These teachers often 'role modelled' a level of interest in a subject that may otherwise appear without purpose, or as boring, and did so in a way which proved inspiring to the younger person. They engaged children actively by their teaching style, and were respectful of the results achieved by them[132]. The challenges provided by the teachers were carefully paced with the skill level already achieved by the young person[133]. The influential teacher demonstrated an individual concern and caring for the young person, providing additional activities which allowed a development of skill[134]. A common theme that ran through this work is that the teachers recognised a talent in the young person, and, with these other factors, drew out that ability[135].

The power and contribution of these teachers was seen as crucial. Csikszentmihalyi and his colleagues[136] see the contribution of the teacher as an inevitable and essential practicality - the young person's ability must be guided by adults "greatly gifted in the ability to catalyse potential into durable achievement". Csikszentmihalyi[137] states this even more directly: "talented children can grow into talented adults only by metabolising the attention of parents, teachers, coaches, mentors ....". Albert[138] describes the impact of teachers on the exceptional individual: working with these individuals opens them to the "crystalizing experience", the 'aha' experience that leads to a commitment to a particular type of work and career - which provides them with support to sustain their aspirations and involvement in this work - and which through this relationship creates a "reality-based sense of identity and competence".

The contribution provided by teachers is also found in and extended by other adults. In research sources they are described as influential adults, role models, or mentors.

Encounters with such adults often occur in the lives of eminent and talented individuals. Walberg et al[139] highlights the different types of adults who may act in this role. Ochse[140] highlights that there was a "plentiful supply" of adults who acted as role models, commonly occupying "prominent and responsible positions in the community". Simonton[141] argues that *the larger the number of role models for "possible imitation" the greater the impact on creative development.* Torrance[142] describes the frequency with which mentors are found (46% of participants in a study), and how this proved one variable which correlated with creative achievement. Also using the term "sponsor" or "patron", he described their contribution as: "Regardless of their own views, (they) encourage and support talented individuals in expressing and testing their ideas .... They protect individuals from the counter-reactions of their peers long enough to permit them to try out some of their ideas. They keep the structure of the situation open enough so that the originality can occur".

There are a limited number of variables within the early years that are known to facilitate the development of talent and creativity. Crucial amongst these appear to be socio-economic status, certain parental characteristics, the quality of relationships with parents, and relationships with influential adults or role models[143].

The standards of education and the pressure to achieve a conformity or norm, generally a low one, within the school environment are thought to inhibit the translation of a gift into an active talent and creativity[144].

Helson[145] speculates that before the young person can develop creative ability they need to arrive at an identity that is clearly separate from the parents – and that the child must be supported in this separate identity. This is, perhaps, the issue that creates the perspective that parents are unlikely to be mentors as well. A parent is having to provide so much in terms of structure and development for a child, how can they also provide a psychological space that gives a child the openness to choose in this kind of way? The Helson study argued that this was quite possible and achievable, albeit that the participants in the study reported a sense of insecurity in having this openness of choice. It was as if the participants believed they had to follow what others laid down and were struggling with the possibility they did not.

A startling perspective contained in research on the development of gifted children[146] suggests that unless this pattern of influence continues, the developmental trajectory can falter as the young person moves into adulthood and a career. Therefore the presence of the mentor in adult years becomes equally powerful and crucial.

An underlying theme that I perceive in my review of how creativity develops the years of childhood and adolescence is expressed by John-Steiner[147]: "New work is born out of the playfulness of the young, and the freshness of perception that does not wilt after childhood. But the process of growth from exploration to the actual construction of a body of work is prolonged, and it entails manifold links between the childish and the most disciplined and purposeful efforts of which human beings are capable." It is in this second area where growth and mentoring in the adult years play a central part in the realisation of individual potential.

Mentoring in the Adult Years

To learn a skill and capitalise on a talent, some form of support from others is necessary for purposes like instruction, encouragement and mentoring[148]. The nature of the contribution of these influential adults is varied.

Keinanen and Gardner,[149] drawing on the social systems perspective of creativity and mentoring, propose that mentoring can be differentiated into 'vertical' or 'horizontal' mentoring. 'Vertical mentoring' seeks to achieve an "uninterrupted transmission of ideas and practices", a "codified technique or tradition" that is "resistant to transformation" and the mentor's task is to pass on the "structure and needs of practice". An example of vertical mentoring is the established sciences, where work can be focused on a small number of laboratories. 'Horizontal mentoring' takes place in work areas where the intent is to "change an existing body of knowledge" and would be more associated with innovation and change. Keinanen and Gardner suggest that work areas like new sciences or computer sciences will be more associated with horizontal mentoring because "no established body of knowledge can be passed on". They suggest that mentoring in this area will be looser, because an individual may be choosing from multiple possible influences or sources of inspiration. They propose that individual characteristics will influence our choice of work areas, for example, a more change-oriented person might well be drawn to an area where horizontal mentoring takes place.

Keinanen and Gardner's work focuses on domains of knowledge and skill where substantial creativity might occur, and 'domain changing action' could be the outcome. However, my view of the body of literature that exists in the study of creative individuals is that it appears oriented towards 'horizontal' mentoring and a potentially democratic relationship between mentor and mentee, in which the latter grows in their own individuality and capability. Against that background, this review proceeds to discuss mentoring activity with that apparent intention.

There are many books and stories about creative people. Reading them is one of my great pleasures, and a means of learning about creative attitudes, perspectives and working practice. 'Apprentice to Genius' is the title of a book by Robert Kanigel [150] describing the 'master apprentice' working relationship that has existed between a remarkable group of scientists. These are men who have achieved great breakthroughs, and proceed to teach others how to do the same. In my own review of literature I find it striking how many stories about mentors are associated with scientists and scientific work. Yet I believe the beauty of the stories is such that many of the perspectives and approaches can be transferred into other disciplines.

The passion of these men (described by Kanigel) for their work meant that for many it was an act of love and play to be able to do what they did.

While the individuals described in his book undoubtedly learned the expertise of science I would infer they were also learning what Teresa Amabile would call the component of creativity, described by Kanigel as a 'style of thinking'. Through so many of the stories you detect an atmosphere or pleasure or joy in the work.

Core within that style of thinking, and reflecting sections above, was a "sense of the significant, or important, or right problem". Relating to the Einstein example, they were learning to identify "the question".

Within the discipline of science they were being taught, according to Kanigel, to balance key questions with techniques that made them approachable or soluble. Yet there was a paradox or contradiction in this step: a technique may *not* be available to solve a problem. *Or* one could identify a "simple, elegant, pointed experiment" that would indicate whether you were on the right track.

Zuckerman's [151] frequently cited work on scientific Nobel laureates provides a further detailed articulation both of the contexts and contribution of the role model and influential adult. She makes clear that these eventual laureates knew enough of their domain of work to seek out both the institution and person with whom they wished to work and study – that they "had a discriminating eye for the masters of their craft as well as for the major universities … doing work at the frontiers of the field". Their role model, in turn, actively sought out bright and able individuals to join them in their work. The future laureates not only gained detailed knowledge from their "master", they acquired a socialisation. This included "more than is ordinarily understood by education or by training: it involves acquiring norms and standards, the values and attitudes, as well as the knowledge, skills and behaviour patterns associated with particular statuses and roles". Through this, the future laureates gained the ability to assess their own work to demanding standards, and became "even more confident of their own abilities than before". Subotnik and Steiner [152] summarise the contribution of the influential adult as moving the younger person from being "the novice to expert".

Gardner [153] proposes both affective and cognitive influences in the shape of another person able to act as a "confidant". This would be someone who would offer unconditional support (affective) and an understanding (cognitive) that explored and gave feedback on the nature of their work.

Two studies by Dean Simonton [154] provide further indications, albeit tentative, of the influence of older adults in the context of the younger person. In his study of 772 artists, Simonton evaluated the influence of a range of relationships found in the social context, these being "paragons, masters, parents, rivals, collaborators, associates, friends, co-pupils, siblings, apprentices and admirers". Paragons ("those whom the artist admired, imitated, emulated, copied, idolised or was otherwise influenced by") and associates ("acquaintances, contacts, fellow members of movements or societies but who could not be considered rivals, collaborators, co-pupils, friends or siblings") emerged as the most influential on the eminence of the artist. In the case of the paragons it does raise the implication that an eminent person can be influenced by individuals they have not had direct contact with.

Daniel Levinson, in his seminal studies of adult lifespan development, articulated the role of the mentor in a breadth of 'plain language' that applied to everyday life, not only the lives of the gifted and exceptionally creative individual[155]. He saw the mentor as a person several years older, and of greater experience and seniority. This relationship had the capacity to become one of "the most complex and developmentally important". He saw the role of the mentor as informal:

- A teacher who enhanced skills and intellectual development.
- A sponsor to facilitate entry.
- A host and guide who welcomed the newcomer to their area of work.
- An exemplar, for the rules and achievements of a domain of work.
- A counsellor for moral support at times of stress.
- A protector of a younger person as they ventured into the uncertainties of a new area of work.

The mentor supported the younger person in finding and relating to a 'dream' of their own. The mentor would believe in the person they mentored, sharing a dream, and "giving it his blessing".

Levinson identifies a crucial aspect of the mentor's role that in the stories he learnt was sometimes forgotten. The mentor's function is transitional. The values underpinning it were, Levinson perhaps surprisingly believed, those of love. The act of mentoring to a mentor is potentially a demand and a strain that take energy and a centreing on personal values in order to deliver this consistently over time. Levinson et al report that mentoring relationships commonly end badly, being clumsily or ungraciously ended by the person being mentored. There are, however, practical reasons for this occurrence – for an individual to act on their developmental experience there comes a point where they must move forward alone. They must take responsibility for themselves. The energetic 'parenting' action must cease, and the young person must move into their own action and life. Perhaps unsurprisingly this break, this moving on, was often done in an atmosphere of difficulty, with the mentor being left with feelings of rejection. Mentors can facilitate that step by accepting and anticipating the need for the person being mentored to depart.

A practical acknowledgement in exploring research work on mentoring is how much of it is based on the experiences of men. Levinson's (1996) study was one of 45 women. His work in life span development psychology is hugely influential, yet this is clearly a small research sample. In contrast to the experience of men he studied, the reports of women are more often negative. Fewer women found a mentor and established a mentoring relationship. Where they occurred, they were with men as mentors and in the social conditions of the time of his study the effect of something like the 'glass ceiling' seemed to be present. Men in the circumstances explored, it seemed, did not believe women would achieve in the same manner as their male counterparts. Levinson writes descriptively of the male mentor: "He usually did not have an intuitive sense of the (woman's) Dream, however articulated or inchoate it might be. He had difficulty giving his blessing to her highest aspirations and making her feel truly welcome within his broader occupational world. Most women, in turn, found it difficult to entertain such ambitions. The barriers to empathy and identification often prevented the development of a fuller mentoring relationship." The lack of female mentors within his study was a reflection of their absence from the more senior levels of occupational hierarchies. Where they were found he also suggested mentoring was sometimes not offered. Levinson saw one of the reasons for this lack of support to an inter-generational conflict which he appeared to consider common in most historical periods.

Harvard psychologist Howard Gardner undertook a ground-breaking study of what was involved in finding 'Good Work'[156] in different occupations. He suggested that what had to be learnt fell into two areas, reflecting both the domain of knowledge as well as the context of work, such as the organisation.

- The domain of knowledge would comprise knowledge, skill, practices, rules values seen in different codes of ethics and work.
- The field or context of work had three major roles – those of the gatekeeper for entry, the expert practitioners and the 'apprentices' or students.

In one of the occupations he studied (genetic scientists) he summarised what he considered the 'experts' modelled for their 'apprentices':
- The thrill of scientific enquiry.
- The pleasure of working with particular materials.
- Creative and quality thinking.
- Integrity and honesty in work.
- Openness to openness – a free flow of information, openness to experience and receptiveness to the unexpected.
- A capacity to form and work to 'dreams' – integrating both ideas *and* scientific disciplines of work.
- Responsibility – to society, the domain of knowledge, others and oneself.

In my own PhD research examining the developmental trajectory of creativity over an individual's lifetime I was surprised to learn the more an individual was acknowledged for their creative activity the more they also described the influence of others on them. The more they were acknowledged as individuals the greater the number of others they cited as mentors, teachers and individuals of influence. It was as if they searched out people to learn from, or were open to learn in a way that attracted others to coach, mentor or teach them. It is this stylistic approach that leads me to offer the concept of these individuals starting a process of self-mentoring. I believe this is a development or extension of the practice described by Zuckerman where individuals seek out their own mentor.

I offer a diagrammatic summary, as follows:

Attitudes and Values of the Mentor

'Attitude' towards Self

Being oneself.
Role modelling such things as
pleasure in work, work as 'play',
time for others, standards of
work, priorities.

Attitude towards the 'mentee'

Person-focused.
Individual concern.
Language for talent.
Belief.

Actions of the Mentor

Shaping and containing a work space

Freedom to explore and learn.
Support in finding own interests.
Challenges paced with skills.
Sends the mentee in search of their own story.
Finding their own choices or 'dream'.
Teaching 'flow'.
Seeking 'the crystallizing experience'.
Clearly, specifically sharing ideas.

Roles

Sponsor
Teacher
Exemplar
Coach
Protector
Supporter
Host

Why Mentor

*"Observing just behind the words, not just surfaces. Glimpsing
and authenticating the inner world, recognising the
hidden beauty, the hidden soul, the hidden gold".*

Phil Cousineau

Developing a relationship that will draw this out.

In closing an exploration of mentoring, there is a more 'poetic' and mythical perspective that I believe is of value and one that reflects the 'deep structure' or values most likely to enhance the act of mentoring another person. Phil Cousineu described the mentor in a reflective book on the power of myth. He believed that in looking back into its mythical and linguistic origins we see the 'mentor' as "mind-maker", someone who helps a younger person make up his own mind, and even re-mind them of their own destiny. (p148.) In strikingly poetic language he writes:

> *"the mentor is the one who is observing just behind the words, not just seeing surfaces, but glimpsing and authenticating a young person's inner world, recognising the hidden beauty, the hidden soul, the hidden gold. Hidden out of self-protection and developing a relationship that draws this out. (...) The mentor is the one who is there to help you light your own fire, unfold your own myth. True mentorship draws out your mind, draws out your hidden qualities, puts the bellows to your soul, fans the flame, develops the gold that the mentor is trying to draw out."*

Cousineau reminded us in the earliest appearance of the 'mentor' in the myth of the Odyssey 'mentor' was the goddess Athena in disguise. If we interpret the image and symbol it reminds us that, like Athena, the mentor is both a balance of the rational, woven with the capacity and skill of the feminine, the insightful, the caring. Cousineau believed that it was the spirit of Athena that infuses the person being mentored with a 'new spirit', a 'new dream' guiding him to become more thoughtful (p120). Cousineau saw Athena as personifying self-counsel, which is, perhaps, another way of moving towards the spirit of self-mentoring.

My speculation is that when we receive the recognition of the mirror of another, we then find the strength and the means to offer that support to ourselves, via 'self-mentoring'. Yet Keinanen and Gardner's work suggests more influences are in action; that in environments where creativity, innovation or change may be accepted, an openness or democracy in ideas and influence develops that prompts individuals to embrace learning and change from many sources.

Let us look at what that means.

Self-Mentoring

Creative individuals, from early stages in their career appear to 'self-mentor', or adopt a self-managing, open approach to sources of influence and learning. Within the life stories of individuals seen as 'gifted' in childhood, there is also an occurrence of those gifts not being carried through and made 'active' in adulthood. As we seek to develop ourselves, what practices might allow us to 'self-mentor'? This action takes on different forms. In a confidence in their own skill, these individuals appear to have a sense of perspective on how they wish to develop, and seek out peers or older skilled individuals who may support and shape their development. These individuals are open to developmental influence in many forms, even at a distance – and reflect on teachers, trainers, authors and public figures who have added some aspect to their personal understanding and performance. There appears to be a personal openness to learning, a driving of learning, and the experience of learning as a way of being.

My summary of the kind of actions I perceive is as follows:

Creating space for the work
and growth that is 'vital'.

Learning passion for one's
calling is 'play' not 'work'.

Find a subject you care about
and love. Choose to work on
that which is 'vital' for your
energy and being.

Self Mentoring?

Care for oneself
and one's needs.

Learning working
practices that support
development and creativity.

Seek out 'teachers'
These could be people, books, work examples or locations.
Be watchful. Stay open to people and material that will
teach you, change you and support your growth.

Reflective questions:
What influential adults have affected your own development?

What was it about them that helped or supported you?

*Are those behaviours or ways of thinking ones that you can 'give' or adopt towards yourself? Let those
behaviours or ways of thinking become ways you support yourself.*

*Are there individuals around you that you would wish to relate to as mentors? Would you be able to
ask them for that form of support?*

*Are there individuals at a distance that might have a mentoring impact on your life? What is it about
them that you admire or that might support your development? In what way can you give that support
to yourself, or learn about it from other sources, such as books?*

As you look at the summary of self-mentoring, in what way can you offer that to yourself?

Conclusions

Mentoring may be described as an activity and a set of behaviours. My belief is that mentoring
is far deeper and more influential than an 'activity' or behaviours alone. Fundamentally I
believe mentoring involves 'seeing' what might be 'in' another person. The mentor will see,
hear, sense the 'mentee' reaching towards a personal dream and aspiration, perhaps only on the
fringes of the younger person's consciousness or awareness. I also believe there may be a beautiful
'psychodynamic' quality to mentoring. The mentor may see or sense a possible unfolding or

development in the other person. Yet the person being mentored, in the pattern that exists in them actually being drawn to a mentor, may also be seeing an aspect of themselves in the mentor that they wish to develop in themselves. The environment being created of acceptance, safety, support for growth, even 'love' reflects that advocated by Carl Rogers for positive personality development, and by his daughter Natalie in her work on the growth of personal creativity.

Mentoring is core in what allows a skill and way of working to be passed from one generation to another, and in that action the mentor is seeding or parenting the work that may follow. Common to the stories of mentors is the sense they are completing a circle, they are passing on something that they received some years before. My own sense, common to writers such as Howard Gruber, Howard Gardner and Mihalyi Csikszentmihalyi, is that enhancing the skill to face the challenging problems in the world today is central to our own survival.

Mentoring also reflects what is believed to be a crucial stage in adult development, known as 'Generativity' (Erikson 1958 and 1980). For those of us who have been fortunate enough to establish and consolidate a career, when we enter our 40s we are challenged to nurture and develop the next generation. Having established our 'self', paradoxically we can spend time giving it away in support to those younger than ourselves. In the formidable Grant Study of Adult Development, psychiatrist George Vaillant describes biology as 'flowing down hill' to the next generation, "putting more into the world than was there before". In this remarkable longitudinal study, Vaillant is also specific that when we can achieve this, it supports a healthier quality of aging for ourselves.[157]

The next chapter turns to explore how creativity may appear or change as we age. It is, perhaps, one of our limited views that we believe creativity declines with age. Each new age brings new psychological tasks and possibilities, and changes to our creative process, finding creativity for the first time, or choosing to return to a possibility of creativity that we saw years ago, are possibilities at any time of our life.

Chapter 4: How Might 'Creativity' Change As We Age?

"The main pathology of later years is our idea of later years. ... We can't imagine aging's beauty because we look only through the eyes of physiology."
(Hillman 1999: pg xx and 16).

Introduction

My fascination with creativity was a two-part question: how does creativity appear in one's life, and what happens to creativity as we age? At the time I was drawn to these questions (the mid-1990s) the most widely accepted academic view was one of 'decline' with age. I suspected there was more to this story. The literature I read and the life stories I heard convinced me of this, and of the presence of what I described in the preface as the 'creative spiral'. We have the opportunity to choose and enter creative work at any age. Where I have seen this happen, as I indicated in chapter 1, I have witnessed an energy and vitality in the individual, a stronger sense of who they are as individuals; I have watched a willingness to make new life choices, to learn a new skill with patience, and grow that skill with a willingness to accept both successes and failures. Society's pressure for success and speed seems to loosen its grip. What I have seen conveys some of the beauty and possibility that come with aging.

I believe our views in western society about aging are quite muddled and lead to confusion in us as individuals. We struggle to increase life-span, fight disease and illness, delay death – and deny aging, discriminate against the older person, and often deprive them of work and contribution. Society appears to want longer life yet have a deep discomfort with what its contents and meaning might be. The struggle seems so often to appear young even though we are not, and resist what we may need to learn and experience in aging.

The last 30 years have seen some remarkable work involved in learning the meaning and possibilities of aging[158]. While the task is incomplete, particularly against the backdrop of the tensions in society I describe above, some beautiful insights have emerged from long term studies, particularly the Grant Study of adult development.

Our first 20 years of adulthood have been described as both apprenticeship and the time in which we choose, grow and form the outward physical and relational choices of our adult years, particularly in the context of what our 'society' wants of us. This involves the development of relationships and career. Somewhere around the age of 40 many of us review the choices and experiences that have made us who we are up to that time. George Vaillant suggested that the inner voices we have responded to up to that time are primarily driven by society and our parents. Deepak Chopra described it in a challenging manner as the "hypnosis of social conditioning"[159]. The midlife phase of life may be the first occasion in which our own true voice emerges from within.

If we examine some of these milestone works in both life-span psychology *and* explorations of creativity and aging, powerful and moving messages emerge about the changes we may experience as we age. These messages offer us a form of hope and shape that the stereotypes of society do not. In writing this review I am setting out to give a summary of what we might experience as we age *and* the possible impact on creativity and a creative life. I believe we may not understand the part, 'aging', without the overview of the whole, 'creativity and aging'.

This chapter:
- Describes the psychological understanding of the midlife decade experience (the time many people seem to feel aging has begun).
- Considers the influences of creativity up to and including middle age.
- Describes its possible impact on creative work in 'middle age' itself.
- Explores subsequent patterns of creative activity in later years.

My goal, as elsewhere in this book, is to offer shape, form, and language for our experience that might be a compass to a landscape which you or others wish to navigate.

Summary of key points:
There is psychological evidence that argues we reach a period in our lives at approximately aged 40 where we significantly reassess our circumstances. The re-evaluation potentially creates a 'confrontation' with aspects of our life structure not serving the direction we desire, and the opportunities that may exist to change.

A number of authors also refer to the realisation in the individual that some parts of their selves have not been 'lived-out' as a consequence of the life chosen to-date. This may lead to new choices being made, or a re-making of earlier life decisions, and choosing new directions. The energy and excitement this can create is startling to witness.

For those already involved in a creative activity this might involve:
- *Continuing creative activity.*
- *Changing to a new area / domain of work.*
- *Broadening an existing work focus to include different questions or possibilities.*

For those who turn to a creative activity for the first time during this age range, this may involve:
- *Choosing an activity to learn.*
- *Choosing an activity to learn that was an aspiration held earlier in life.*
- *Being willing to use work practices common to creative individuals, such as being willing to learn, to fail and learn again at a place appropriate to them.*
- *Feeling freed from some of the expectations of others and society more generally, and able to make new choices as a result.*

'The Late Life Style'?
The Late Life Style is a phenomenon that has been noticed in the older years of creative individuals. It seems that the experiences of aging and personal mortality become part of and explored through the creative work, e.g. expressing and exploring the experience of illness. The work produced may become simpler and expressed more directly in this time period.

Other patterns that may appear?
A comprehensive study of creative individuals suggests that, even when in older years they keep working on creative projects, often with a reduced anxiety or concern for performance. The fascination with their chosen work continues, and more projects remain to be accomplished.

Experiences of Aging

The Midlife Period

In different forms of literature the ages 35 – 45 have been termed the 'midlife decade'. With changing patterns of health and longevity within society it is conceivable that this could be seen as outdated, i.e. that a 'midlife' period now occurs at a later age. However, there seems evidence from many sources that a distinct form of psychological 'shift' begins in this approximate time period. This 'shift' can re-orientate or redirect many of us.

My own experience of this period felt initially like confusion and chaos. Adapting a phrase made famous by Joseph Campbell – "I was climbing a ladder which I then realised was up against the wrong wall". This experience was central to bringing me to the questions I explore in this book.

The midlife decade and the transition seen within it have emerged as a recognised period of adult development[160]. The interest and research in the midlife period dates from the 1960s approximately, with a peak of interest demonstrated in the literature occurring between 1965 and 1980. The relative recency of this interest in this area can be understood in the context of a life expectancy in 1900 being 50 years old, compared to 70 years for males in 1980 and 78 for females[161], with these life-expectancies still changing. The interest in the midlife period can also be seen as an evolution of the work of Sigmund Freud in childhood, and Anna Freud and Erik Erikson on youth, adolescence and the adult life span. In the early 1970s, there were relatively few conceptualisations of development in adulthood. Neugarten and Gould argued there was an assumption that the issues salient to childhood were projected forward into this time[162].

Daniel Levinson[163] proposed that our 20s were a form of 'apprentice adulthood' where we made and tested our choices for an adult life. He saw our 'life structure' as comprising a small number of large choices, such as occupation, relationships and home location. The late 20s and early 30s were a period in which we either adjusted those choices, or consolidated and developed them. George Vaillant, writing from the longitudinal Grant Study of adult development[164], built on Erik Erikson's theories of the adult Life Cycle. He drew similar conclusions to Levinson, identifying a period of career consolidation, and intimacy with others in this age group.

Levinson[165] proposed the midlife transition was a five-year period from 40 – 45 years old, with a small variance in the ages at which midlife was experienced. However, others argue for a longer period of focus[166]. This chapter will, therefore, look at a full decade at least that becomes pivotal to the quality of aging that follows in order to embrace these wider views.

A number of general adult development studies have also considered the role of creativity in this time period.   One of the earliest articles concerning the midlife[167] examined it from the standpoint of the impact on the creative lives of artists.   The work of Levinson et al also comments on the potential impact of midlife on creative work.

This decade is called a "transition" by some, a "crisis" by others.   The perspective of a crisis occurring in this period has undoubtedly come from some of the journalistic publications of the work on this period, which appears to have slanted the understanding of the meaning of this life period[168].   This review focuses on this period as a *transition*.   A transition is defined as: " … a change which moves the person from one position or stage to another"[169], which may involve various psychological and social adaptations[170].   For Levinson it also included elements of ending and beginning, or initiation with an underlying move towards "individuation" [171].   While the principal theorists use the word "transition", they also acknowledge that a crisis can occur for some within a transition.   There is a debate, which will be reviewed later in this section, on whether the midlife transition is a phenomenon or phase experienced by everyone.   Jaques' classic influential article on this subject suggests that it is an experience "which manifests in some form with everyone".

The Characteristics of the Midlife Transition

This period is described as containing a range of possible experiences that are physical, psychological and social in origin.   This review will focus on the psychological affects.   There is a high degree of commonality of the descriptions contained in the earlier and more recent literature.   No single event or occurrence is recognised as the starting point of the transition, and they may be experienced in any order.   While these characteristics represent the way the experience of the midlife transition is reported, more recently[172] they are being written of as reflecting the "multiple meanings of age" – the ways in which it will be encountered and experienced.   A range of possible midlife characteristics will be looked for in this review.

Many of the most cited characteristics of the midlife transition in literature are psychological or internally experienced.   The focus on psychological characteristics and experience is a part of the life course or life cycle perspective on adult development[173].   The physical and the psychological characteristics are theorised as interacting[174].

Vaillant, interestingly, likens the midlife transition to a second adolescence[175].   He implies that some part of us begins to realise that we have trodden a path up to this point that society and our social group has expected of us.   The reflection that this transition implies involves a reassessment of the experiences of many aspects of life to-date.

Carl Jung describes the essence that I have seen in others: *"Many – far to many – aspects of life which should have been experienced lie in the lumber-room along with dusty memories; but sometimes, too, they are glowing coals under grey ashes".[176]*   The choices we made, which involved some experiences being given precedence over others, may get revisited.   The choices we did *not* make may call to us.

This period of re-evaluation has a number of potential sources.   There is often a practical recognition of what has been described as the "aspirations – achievements gap"[177].   The hopes and plans from early adult life and career are weighed against what has actually been achieved.   For many individuals there is a gap between the two which has two implications.   First, the realisation of what has been achieved compared with what the individual hoped and was possible.   There might have been a failure to reach aspirations despite their efforts, or a failure to attempt or risk what is necessary to attain them. Second, what opportunities, if any, exist for closing the gap between aspirations and achievement in the time remaining to the individual[178]?

A number of authors[179] also refer to the realisation in the individual that some parts of their selves have not been 'lived-out' as a consequence of the life chosen to-date. The causes may be practical, such as the demands of career or family, or social, such as following of traditions or restrictions that exist in the individual's context. "Some parts of oneself have been neglected in the maturation process and some parts may never be fulfilled"[180]. Whatever the cause, there is a possible weighing-up or comparison of the person they have become in comparison with the individual they dreamed of being earlier in adult life.

The experience of this stage also, suggests Erik Erikson, provides an impetus or questioning for how the individual might nurture or develop the next generation. This might be a concern for the growth and leadership of those with us or working for us; the development of individuals that form the next generation or creative products or work that may influence them[181]. Neugarten[182] uses an unusual expression for this that I love, in describing the task as involving the "creation of social heirs".

Of a more direct and difficult nature is an experience or realisation that 'death' has become a personal reality to the individual. Elliot Jaques[183] discusses one of the paradoxical experiences of the midlife in describing the recognition that as we enter what in many respects may be a "prime" of life, "… the prime and fulfilment are dated. Death lies beyond …". Death has changed from being a concept to a personal matter[184].

With or without a more personal experience of death, one of the commonest reported experiences of the midlife transition is a changing orientation to time. As the individual reaches a time approximating to an anticipated midpoint in life, time is restructured into a sense of time-left-to-live rather than a time since birth. Another potentially galvanising way in which it has been stated is "there is only as much time left in the future as there is time in the past"[185]. One of the consequences of this in the individual is a recognition that not all that had been hoped-for in the life span will be accomplished, that only a finite amount can be achieved and that much may have to remain unfinished and unrealised. This is described as a creating a sense of 'time-urgency'[186].

The awareness of death also relates to one of the other commonest reported experiences – an awareness of the polarities that exist in life, and that one of our deepest challenges is to acknowledge and reconcile these opposites. For example, Jaques describes it as a realisation that life and mortality exist together, and that this can be mitigated by the positive element of the polarity, by the will to live life. A further perspective that he describes is: "beliefs in the inherent goodness of man are replaced by a recognition and acceptance of the fact that inherent goodness is accompanied by hate and destructive forces within, which contribute to man's own misery and tragedy"[187]. McAdams[188] also describes a shift from a belief in "absolute truths" to truths that are situationally specific.

Several authors describe a change in personal priorities as occurring at this time. Kets de Vries talks of an increased preoccupation with the inner life, introspection, reflection and self-evaluation. For McIlroy it is an existential questioning of the self, values and life itself. In practical terms it is a taking stock, a seeing of one's self in realistic terms – and depression sometimes results because of shortfalls and disappointments[189].

The work of the midlife transition is involves a facing, confrontation and accommodation of some or all of the experiences described above. These experiences constitute potential "psychological turning points" – defined by Moen and Wethington[190], after Clausen, as "a new insight into one's self, a significant other or important life situation; this insight becomes a motive that leads to redirecting, changing or improving one's life". The turning points take place against a background of a changed sense of reality, of time ahead, and personal mortality. Levinson also argues that these experiences constitute "individuation", a growing exploration and sense of who the individual is as a person, what they want, as well as what the realities of the world and life are really like. The midlife transition is the process of reconciliation of gaps in the life structure, and the actions that are needed to close them.

A Perspective of Creative Work in Middle Age

This section first explores what academic literature suggests about patterns in creative work at the midlife and in middle age. It will then incorporate ideas and insights from other sources related to the general population.

The literature on creativity produced in the period 1950 – 1980 appears to have created a potentially stereotypical message that "creativity declines with age". Even if there is a stereotype, the evidence that "creative achievement becomes more infrequent with advancing adult age cannot be ignored"[191]. However, the contents and meaning of the earlier literature has now been considered in more depth and proves more complex than this simple conclusion.

The identified age-related decline is an average of the patterns found in many disciplines[192]. This being the case, there will be some disciplines where the peak and decline is earlier, some later. Lindauer's work on artists, for example, portrays a peak to the curve in this field that potentially occurs in the mid-forties or later. Dean Simonton[193] argues from the standpoint of his extensive research that for some individuals the curve will not decline at all. Therefore, global statements about peaks in creativity occurring at a certain age range are misleading.

Simonton[194] has taken the exploration of the potential meanings of an apparently declining performance curve further by using a mathematical perspective. By calculating the area under the curve he argues that the post-peak period of work represents over half of that available to the individual in the span of their career. The declining curve does not, for example, remove creativity – the decline in creativity will not make the creative person uncreative – ample scope for work remains. In the seventh decade work output may still be approximately 50% of the peak, and exceeding that of the first decade of work, the twenties. Therefore, any age decline does not make a person devoid of creativity[195]. As the curve represents an average this will of course conceal very wide individual variations and individual creators may show very different patterns. Simonton acknowledges there will be many examples available which prove an exception to these principles. Therefore, we are not considering the possible presence or absence of creativity in this time period, but the characteristics of change that may occur to creative activity in this age range.

There are, however, further patterns within output and achievement to be acknowledged. Three common patterns occur within output of the exceptional creative individual – starting work early, i.e. prodigiousness in childhood, production at extraordinary rates during the career, and working until late in life[196]. Therefore, late life potential and activity is heavily associated with early potential[197]. Simonton also argues that output and achievement are linked. "Quality of output is strongly associated with quantity, i.e. most productive periods are, on average, the same periods in which the most successful pieces emerge"[198]. Simonton charted the work curves associated with major and minor work and suggested that "they are basically identical – the period of most masterpieces will also see the most easily forgotten work". For this reason, he argues that continuing output and potential can still lead to significant achievement in later years.

One of the principal reasons proposed for declining achievement and output with age is that of ill health. Nowadays, interference of extrinsic factors can be mitigated with advances in modern medicine[199].

There is also some evidence that in certain cases productivity can undergo a renaissance in the later years. This work does not take output and achievement back to midlife levels, but it does indicate and argue for a potential in later life even when output levels lessen in quantity.

Outcomes of the Midlife Transition and Their Impact on Creative Work

There are alternative interpretations about the impact of midlife experiences on creative work in 'middle-age', as well as the characteristics of work itself. This section explores both factors.

Different authors write about the way in which the midlife transition experiences " … challenge us to recreate our identities in ways that enhance our sense of unity and purpose in life"[200]. This involves the individual working through unresolved problems of earlier life or revising beliefs and goals for the future[201].

This means that the re-evaluation and assessments described create a confrontation with aspects of the life structure not serving the direction desired by the individual and the opportunities that may exist to change. These may be parts of the life structure, such as job or relationships, or attitudes and values that have been developed or taken on in adult life[202]. An individual may review an existing 'life-structure' or seek to recreate life choices that were not made or taken at earlier ages. Gould also suggests that working on these issues leads to a quality of "heaviness" that can characterise the midlife transition; the results or subsequent decisions can represent its associated growth or 'flowering'.

The common themes that emerge from reported experiences of the mid-life transition are[203]:

- A personal questioning and re-evaluation, and changes in the individual's sense of self.

- A recognition or awareness of the commencement of physical decline.

- A recognition of personal mortality - or the ceasing of its denial.

- A recognition of personal needs, hopes and ambitions in contrast to those which have hitherto been 'imposed' in some way externally.

- A new sense of 'time' being limited, and of work or actions the individual seeks to accomplish in the time remaining to him/her.

- A questioning of what form living may take in the time remaining, of what action or behaviours to devote oneself to, and attempts to reshape or redirect one's life accordingly.

There are a number of outcomes of mid-life transitional experiences that may be seen in creative work. Jaques, having reviewed hundreds of biographies, makes several proposals, in a seminal paper (1965). He suggests:

- A creative career may come to an abrupt end, for example in the drying up of work.

- Creative capacity may show itself for the first time.

- There may be a decisive change in the content or processes involved in creativeness.

- Changes are characterised or seen in either the mode or method of work, or its content. Jaques suggests that the style of work involves a switch to a "sculpting approach" involving a working and reworking of activity, creating a bigger step between the first inspiration and the finished product. This is in contrast to the intense and spontaneous work that occurs in earlier adulthood.

- Jaques also suggests that the emerging sense of death and the tragic in the individual will be reflected in the work, in place of the "lyrical" work of earlier life.

Further, looking at the longevity of creative work, the earlier a person commenced some form of creative activity in their lifespan, the more changes may be made in the midlife period.

Therefore, rather than looking at the question as solely one of productivity or quality, a range of other characteristics or changes may show themselves. Diagrammatically it may be summarised as follows:

	Process? Early life decisions or choices may be reviewed or changed.		Possible outcomes or developments: Creative work appears for the first time. we need to take the time, courage, and effort to grow this activity (see Chapter 2).
Creative work in Middle Age?	There is an awareness of a growing freedom from social demands and pressures.		Changes may occur to the discipline, content or process of pre-existing creative work.
	In this process we may become aware more strongly of our own 'voice' rather than that society or our social group has asked of us.		'Generativity' may emerge as a form of 'creativity'; the mentoring or nurturance of the younger generation. A gradual emergence of the 'late life style' where creativity becomes a means of exploring the experiences of aging.

'Creativity' and creative work appear for the first time.

Part of our experience of midlife is the re-evaluation of choices previously made, and a life structure that has been developed.   As part of this process we may realise that we are drawn to a creative activity, or that there was one we turned away from years ago, and would wish to re-make that decision.   These choices may reflect some of the possibilities described in chapter 2.   These words are deceptively simple to write, yet the experience described can be profound and energising.

These steps are tentative, and may be undermined by a cultural stereotype that skills are easily learnt and that quality work is done without struggle.   A choice to learn a skill an area of work important to us requires nurturing and patient steps.   The section in Chapter 2 on developing the working habits of creative individuals is an illustration of the choices and actions that may be made in this time.

For those individuals already engaged in some form of creative work, this engagement may have an absorbing quality associated with the characteristics of 'flow' described in Chapter 1 and 2, and therefore provide a source of meaning in life.   Balancing the losses that might be associated with aging, an individual may become more selective in their choices as to what is important to them.   The following midlife experiences may be encountered.

Patterns found in later-life engagement with creative work?

Nakamura and Csikszentmihalyi[204] proposed three principal patterns for those already engaged in creative work.

- Continued activity in a domain.

- A change of domain.
- A broadening of focus within or beyond domains.

I infer that these patterns also evolve, over time, into something else that is a deeper expression of our individual needs and unfolding, which is summarised in the experiences of the 'late life style', described below.   Let us review, first, a summary of Nakamura and Csikszentmihalyi's ideas.

Nakamura and Csikszentmihalyi conclude that the experiences of artists and scientists are different to those of us who work in other disciplines.   Artists and scientists work in a way where much of what they work on is 'self-invented'.   Their patterns of present and future work are uncertain, and must be developed and explored.   For that reason they are already familiar with the experience of working through unstructured uncertainty as an aspect of the challenge of old age; "they have spent a lifetime actively shaping their own experience".

What might those of us in different forms of work experience?   Potentially we, too, may draw energy from our motivation to work in a particular way, or on certain problems.   Alternatively, those of us who enter middle age or later life without that experience of handling uncertainty may be moved by an 'inner calling' to attempt a form of work or self-expression that we previously had chosen not to try.   We face, however, a need that the majority of creative workers must encounter – for the development of the tenacity to stay with a subject or an experience about which we are uncertain or are unclear, and trust that our own effort will bring an outcome into form.

Continued activity in a domain

Nakamura and Csikszentmihalyi[205] describe an individual's on-going involvement in a particular domain in a strikingly focused manner: "the most basic aspect of vital engagement that fosters continued involvement in later life is the very fact that the endeavour has become, over time, a central source of flow and meaning in the person's life.   That is, the relationship with the domain has continued to be absorbing and has come to locate the individual in the world in a way that matters".

The domain is a source of 'meaning' that in itself supports on-going involvement.   This involvement may include the social structure or network with which one is involved, such as peers, teachers or students, or the sense of connection with other creative writers over time.   On-going creative work in a domain of knowledge and skill connects any of us to the history from which that work has emerged *and* the unfolding or horizon towards which it is developing.   The work may be projects, tasks or themes being explored, beloved in their own right, or returned to as new understanding, technological or methodological changes allow.   Seen in this way, the connection, the work is self-renewing and reflects 'meaning' connected to both past and future.

Age can create new roles within this domain of work, such as continuing to study and learn as new developments occur, together with mentoring or sponsoring new learning in the company of others[206].

The experiences that may push a creator from relationship with an existing domain could include reduced health, change in the domain itself, or reduced access in the social context.

A change of domain

Nakamura and Csikszentmihalyi[207] appear to imply that a creator's change of domain is likely to occur due to waning interest,   Alternatively, some individuals will shift domain or sub-domain intentionally or regularly as a means of maintaining involvement.   The shift of domain may take away previous structures of support or sources of meaning. This implication of both gains and losses occurring in the change need to be managed.

Broadening of Focus

A third 'path' of change sits, perhaps, between the previous two. Here, an individual may achieve a change of focus *and* retain contact with the domain of work by reaching for 'broader questions'. For some, Nakamura and Csikszentmihalyi cite detailed activities, such as 'organising knowledge', e.g. writing text books. Yet seen in a wider perspective this change can also have the quality of moving beyond a domain as a discrete source of work, and examining interconnections, e.g. philosophical, social or political. I also link this type of change to the 'late life style' described below.

The interview results from my PhD research, as implied above, suggested possibly simpler patterns. An individual might change the content of their work, either within a domain or to a new one. Alternatively the individual might change the processes by which they work, and in that create a different experience of their domain of activity.

There are, however, further views of possible changes that occur related to the processes and experiences of aging; the late life style.

The 'Late Life Style'

The phenomenon of the Late Life Style offers us a fascinating insight into the possible dynamics and contribution of creativity in later years. In my work with individuals this is what I have most commonly seen.

From a largely theoretical (rather than empirical) position, focused on the work of artists, Cohen-Shalev[208] argued for an examination of what she described as the 'late life style' or the 'old age style'. She proposes that to focus on the quantity of work, or peak and decline, in later life as a measure of what happens to creativity, is inadequate. Some other approach is needed which considers the intrinsic features of the experience of ageing, e.g. the content, form, language, style and variation of work in this time period. Kastenbaum[209] argued a primary focus on achievement and social acclaim means aspects of creativity will go unexamined. Cohen-Shalev pressed for an examination of the "primary aspects" of artistic work "such as themes, formal structure, technique and imagery" in order to go beyond the product-centred perspective of an average of the best years of work.

Cohen-Shalev acknowledged at the time of writing these articles that the empirical implications of these suggestions needed further exploration. She also argued that the failure to examine the changes that occurred in later life represented a prejudice against ageing and the older individual.

She made initial steps at defining shifts in artistic style later in life – but these lack a level of definition that would support empirical work. She wrote, in a manner that reflects the conclusions of midlife researchers, of an increased focus on the interior life, and a withdrawal into "inner circles of experience", and "an increased occupation with the artistic self and the reconsideration of the meaning of art for one's life and humanity at large"[210].

Lindauer[211] extended the examination of late-life concept empirically, again with artists. While acknowledging his findings were not observed in all the artists he examined, he observed three general patterns in late life work: declining reputations, achieving recognition in old age, and artists reputed to have done their best work in old age. Specifically, he found a number of well known artists (e.g. Rembrandt, Michaelangelo, Titian, Goya, and Cézanne) drastically changed their style in later life, with shifts in technique, composition, subject matter and affective tone.

In reviewing the literature of other researchers Lindauer found other contributory definitions to the late life style. "A shift from the dramatic, physical, busy, to the more tranquil, inner-directed and darker visions of the older artist. There is a shift to looser, diffuse, less literal understandings." And: "An inner directed and introspective focus rather than action-oriented because of a withdrawal to the inner world of experience." These words suggest, again, a change in focus or process on the part of the creative individual.

Lindauer speculated on potential reasons for this stylistic shift. Recognising that no single reason was likely to explain this change, he suggested it may be a reflection of life stage, decreased concern with success, failure or material ambitions, and/or a reflection of physical, biological or mental breakdowns which influence the perceptions of sight and colour used by artists. He also supported Simonton in the view that it could, potentially, reflect the artist's understanding of declining years and impending death, and a personal portrayal and working out of these experiences.

Munsterberg[212] in a book that is art-historical, yet quoted in creativity literature, presented a series of case studies which examine the changes to the work of artists that occurred in later life. He described cases where acclaimed work has been produced in old age, as well as the stylistic shifts that can occur in this time. For example, in a study of Michaelangelo's work, he proposed a reason for the style changes: "the artist transcends artistic conventions and gives expression to his most profound and personal sentiments". He argued strongly, for example, that the experience of aging was a source of creative inspiration and material for Michaelangelo. In several other case studies, Munsterberg described work changes that are indicative of changed priorities on the part of the artist, on-going practical and emotional support, and the acknowledgement received in these later years. Simonton[213] also proposed that, even in the face of illness and difficulty, creative individuals like Bach or Handel persisted in creative work in old age. He called this a "self-actualising process" that motivates creative workers to overcome the infirmities of age. There is also evidence that not only can a creative person push through the restrictions of illness in later years, but it can also be a source of creative output, (e.g. the work of Goya in later life[214]).

Munsterberg's studies also concur with the work of Simonton (described earlier): those who worked well in later life were, generally, but not exclusively, those who started their career early.

Simonton adds two further understandings to the characteristics of creative work in later life, in connection with playwrights and musicians. In a 1983 study of 81 Athenian and Shakespearean plays he proposed that the content of plays reflected the age of the authors. Later plays were found to be more concerned with religious or mystical experiences and the role of God in human affairs. "In the dramatist's later years he evidently becomes less concerned with material goods and more committed to spiritual questions". He concluded: "it is almost as if the dramatist, through literary creativity, is working out the big questions that all of us must encounter as the end of our lives draw near".

In a later study of 1919 works of 172 classical composers Simonton[215] reported that the work of the end of life (a) had shorter playing times, (b) lower melodic originality, and (c) enjoyed higher popularity in classical repertories and were rated as more profound by musicologists. In Simonton's expression composers were saying "more with less". Simonton speculated on the source of this change in style. He suggested that, aware of advancing age and their musical hopes in comparison with their achievements, they were seeking "a last artistic testament". This conclusion was echoed by Cohen-Shalev[216] - "works of elderly artists are frequently described as "last utterances", attempts "to solve the enigma of life" - and similarly by Kastenbaum.

Storr[217] links these late life changes in creative style and approach to life span development. He suggested that a creative individual will enter a "third period" of production in the fifties and sixties. (The first period is characterised by learning the craft, and the second by socially influenced production). Working from the perspective that creative work reflects life experiences, Storr describes the third period as more inner-directed, or inner-focused. He suggested a number of characteristics seen in many musical, artistic and literary examples:

- "They are often unconventional in form and (…) striving to achieve a new kind of unity between elements (…)".
- "They are characterised by an absence of rhetoric and any need to convince".
- "They seem to be exploring remote areas of experience which are intrapersonal or suprapersonal rather than interpersonal".

The literature described in this section is indicative of the difficulties of portraying the late life style in enough precision to support empirical examination. This research project does, however, seek data on changes to creative activity in this middle age period (45 – 60 years old) and examine it for characteristics of the late life style.

Further indications from self-report and biographic study

The expression of some form of creativity in middle and later age holds the possibility for learning, expression and meaning. Vaillant's longitudinal study suggests strongly that this expression is related to positive and healthier aging for any of us, whether new to creativity, or maintaining a longer standing relationship.[218]

Csikszentmihalyi's (1996) study of 91 living creative individuals' reports on the experiences of these individuals in "the later years" and adds further optimistic colour and texture to these ideas.

Csikszentmihalyi supported questioning the perception of a decline in creative activity over time described earlier and reported that the productivity of his sample did not decline with age, and that if anything it increased. He also concluded that the capacity to retain quality with quantity was present, and that memorable work may be produced in later life.

The perception of his participants was that their ability to work was largely unimpaired as they aged, and that their goals remained as significant as they had been in earlier life. Complaints about health or well-being were largely absent from his interviews of participants. Attitudes to their physical health were largely positive, despite reports of energy loss and the need to slow down. Twice as many reported positive changes as negative ones. Abilities associated with crystallised intelligence were perceived as increasing, e.g. "making sensible judgements, recognising similarities across different categories, using induction and logical reasoning"[219].

A significant positive development in personal traits was reported as "diminished anxiety over performance, being less driven, exhibiting more courage, confidence and risk-taking". Women reported twice as many positive outcomes as men.

Comments from these participants concerning their relationship to domains of performance were uniformly positive. "It seems the promise of more and different knowledge never lets us down (…) symbolic domains remain always accessible and their rewards remain fresh till the end of life". Csikszentmihalyi acknowledged a contradiction. These individuals were actively and deeply engaged in work they found exciting until very late in life (the eighties and nineties for some participants).   However, the fulfilment of the work many were engaged in would be unattainable to them in the time remaining.   He suggested "these people never run out of exciting goals".   "… there was very little (…) dwelling on past success (…) everyone's energies were focused on tasks still to be accomplished".

Lindauer et al[220] have made an important contribution to articulating what else may be happening to the experience and performance of creativity in later years.   In a questionnaire survey they asked 88 prominent graphic artists in the age range 60s – 80s to review the performance and characteristics of their work over time.   There were consistent reports of positive changes to the quality, quantity and content of creative work well into the 60s, with only marginal declines beyond that time.   The primary reasons described included increased skill and improved techniques that came from on-going learning and the discovery of new working materials; and increase in time available to them due to a decline in family and responsibilities; and an increased "acceptance of themselves, their work and their abilities" – and an acceptance of others.   A "reduced concern with other people's criticisms or evaluations" was also reported as a source of work – the freedoms to attempt work they may have previously have been deterred from trying.   This presents an important contrasting perspective to the recognised peak of social acclaim that occurs commonly in the first half of the 40s.   This research by Lindauer et al could suggest that social acclaim is less of a priority creatively than before – and that other priorities have emerged.

Reflective questions:
What are your experiences of the midlife period, or subsequent middle age?

Are you questioning your 'life structure' (the 3 or 4 main components of your life)?

What 'dreams' did you have in early adulthood?   What have been fulfilled, and which remain?

Did you turn away from a 'dream' in early adulthood, in order to follow an alternative 'path'?

Are you drawn back to that 'dream' now?   What practical ways exist for you to explore its potential in the present?   (E.g. the steps outlined in Chapter 2.)

Conclusions

The possible changes to 'creative' work as we age are deeper, more varied and complex than I believe many of us credit.   We may change the content or process of our work or interests.   We may return to an earlier dream or aspiration of earlier life, not yet fulfilled, and seek to fulfil it now.   I summarise them in the following way:

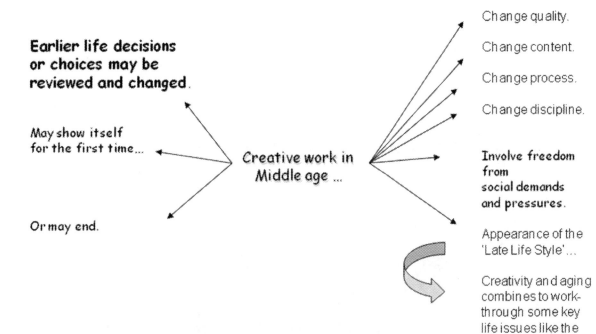

Earlier life decisions or choices may be reviewed and changed.

May show itself for the first time...

Or may end.

Creative work in Middle age ...

Change quality.

Change content.

Change process.

Change discipline.

Involve freedom from social demands and pressures.

Appearance of the 'Late Life Style'...

Creativity and aging combines to work-through some key life issues like the experience of illness and death.

Epilogue: The 'Creative Spiral'

I started to use the phrase 'creative spiral' because of the stories I have heard about creative lives. I found myself believing and seeing that the opportunity to find, develop and change our creativity occurs at many ages through our lifetime. Our lives have structural elements – school days, starting an occupation, becoming a worker or a professional, the mid-life period, middle age – each of which offer us opportunities to choose and re-choose a life path. A decision made at one point can be re-made at another. Choices that were *not* taken at one time can be chosen anew in another time. There are practical implications. Yet choices can be changed, or re-made. We find our own 'voice' and more of it. We loosen the grip of 'social pressure' on our work, each allowing ourselves more freedom than we previously experienced. This can make turning to creative work in later years an act of relaxation and beauty or challenge and excitement.

I believe the key questions at any age are concerned with 'what do you love?' In what activities do you experience a sense of vitality? What activities are you drawn towards or dream of doing? What would you choose to do if you could let go of your worry or concern? What do you sense is a deep reflection of your Self? All these questions give a clue to activities and actions that might bring us energy, vitality, fulfilment and happiness. The wonderful reality is the answers may change, deepen and mature as we age.

Therefore, if you sense the answers to these questions at any age, or you see the energy of a child or younger person in these areas, then the challenge is to have the courage and practical support to take the step. Have the patience to learn a skill. Find teachers that teach in a way that suits you. Seek mentors who affirm your choices and support your learning. These could be 'direct' mentors, present in your life, or even 'distant' mentors, individuals who role-model the actions, beliefs and values that you most need to learn.   Risk 'failure', because this, too, means that you are working at an edge where errors and experiments may help your development.   Do this for yourself, or support it in another person.

I came across two wonderful studies of creativity when doing my research.   Residents of an old people's home in Germany were taught a creative skill (embroidery).   Their use of medication fell, their health as perceived by family members improved.   Maybe this is a message, that creative work at any age has benefits for all of our being.

In writing Chapter 1, I speculated whether 'creativity' was a form of 'play' that kept us flexible, even 'young' in our outlook and being.   The more I explore this subject, the more I believe that it is.   I wonder whether the flow-like experience is also expressed in a few lines of T.S. Eliot's (1944 / 2000) Four Quartets:

> *At the still point, there the dance is, (...)*
> *Where past and future are gathered.*
> *Neither movement from nor towards,*
> *(...) Except for the point, the still point,*
> *There would be no dance, and there is only the dance.*

Creativity is a form of play, at the 'still point' where time appears to stop, which is also a 'dance'.

References

Albert, R. S. (Ed.) (1992) Genius and Eminence. Oxford: Pergamon Press. (Second edition.)

Albert, R.S. (1992a) A Developmental Theory of Eminence. In: Albert, R. S. (Ed.) (1992) Genius and Eminence. Oxford: Pergamon Press. (Second edition.)

Albert, R.S. (1994) The Achievement of Eminence: A Longitudinal Study of Exceptionally Gifted Boys and Their Families. In: Subotnik, R.F. and Arnold, K.D. (eds.) (1994.) Beyond Terman: Contemporary Longitudinal Studies of Giftedness and Talent. New Jersey: Ablex Publishing Corporation.

Albert, R.S. (1996) Some Reasons Why Childhood Creativity Often Fails to Make It Past Puberty into the Real World. In: Runco, M.A. (1996) (Ed.) Creativity from Childhood Through Adulthood: The Developmental Issues. San Francisco: Jossey-Bass Publishers, No. 72, Summer 1996.

Amabile, T.M. (1983) The Social Psychology of Creativity.

Amabile, T.M. (1996) Creativity in Context: (Update to the Social Psychology of Creativity.) USA: Westview Press.

Barron, F. (1988) Putting Creativity to Work. In Sternberg, R.J. (Ed.) The Nature of Creativity. Cambridge: Cambridge University Press.

Bee, H. (1998) Lifespan Development (Second Edition). Harlow, England: Longman.

Bloom, B.S. (1985) Developing talent in young people. New York: Ballentine.

Boden. M. (1999) Computer Models of Creativity. In: Sternberg, R.J. (Ed.) (1999). The Handbook of Creativity. Cambridge: Cambridge University Press.

Bohart, A.C. (2007) The Actualising Person. In: Cooper, M., O'Hara, M., Schmid, P.F. and Wyatt, G. (Eds). (2007) The Handbook of Person Centred Psychotherapy and Counselling. Basingstoke, Palgrave MacMillan.

Brennan, T.P. and Piechowski, M.M. (1991) A Developmental Framework for Self-Actualization. Journal of Humanistic Psychology. 1991, VOL. 31, Pt 3, Summer, p43 – 64.

Brim, O.G., Jr. (1976) Theories of the Male Mid-Life Crisis. Counselling Psychologist. 1976, Vol. 6, p2 – 9.

Cameron, J. (1992) The Artist's Way. London: Pan Books.

Cangemi, J.P. (1976) Characteristics of Self-Actualising Individuals. Psychology. 1976, Vol. 13, pt 2, p48 – 49.

Carr, A. (2004) Positive Psychology: The Science of Happiness and Human Strengths. Hove: Routledge Ltd.

Cohen-Shalev, A. (1986) Artistic Creativity Across the Adult Life Span: An Alternative Approach. Interchange. 1986, Vol. 17, 4, p1 - 16.

Cohen-Shalev, A. (1989) Old Age Style: Developmental Changes in Creative Production from a Life-span Perspective. Journal of Ageing Studies. 1989, Vol. 3, p21 - 37.

Compton, W.C. (2005) An Introduction to Positive Psychology. United States: Thompson Wadworth Publishing.

Cooper, M., O'Hara, M., Schmid, P.F. and Wyatt, G. (Eds). (2007) The Handbook of Person Centred Psychotherapy and Counselling. Basingstoke, Palgrave MacMillan.

Corlett, E.S. and Millner, N.B. (1993) Navigating Mid-life: Using Typology as a Guide. California: Consulting Psychologist Press Books.

Cousineau, P. (2001) Once and Future Myths. Berkeley, CA, Conari Press Books

Craft, A. (2000) Creativity Across the Primary Curriculum: Framing and Developing Practice. London: Routledge Ltd.

Csikszentmihalyi, M. (1975) Beyond Boredom and Anxiety: Experiencing Flow in Work and Play. (25th Anniversary Edition.) San Francisco: Jossey-Bass Publishers.

Csikszentmihalyi, M. and Getzels, J.W. (1988) Creativity and Problem Finding in Art. In Farley, F.H and Neperud, R.W. The Foundations of Aesthetics, Art and Art Education. New Your: Praeger Ltd.

Csikszentmihalyi, M. (1992a) Flow: The Psychology of Happiness. London: Rider Books.

Csikszentmihalyi, M. (1992a) Motivation and creativity. In: Albert, R. S. (Ed.) (1992) Genius and Eminence. Oxford: Pergamon Press. (Second edition.)

Csikszentmihalyi, M. (1994) The Domain of Creativity. In: Feldman, D.H., Csikszentmihalyi, M., and Gardner, H. (1994.) Changing the World: A Framework for the Study of Creativity. London: Praeger.

Csikszentmihalyi, M. (1996) Creativity: Flow and The Psychology of Discovery and Invention. London: Harper Collins.

Csikszentmihalyi, M. (1997) Living Well: The Psychology of Everyday Life. London: Phoenix Books. (Also published in 1997 as "Finding Flow: The Psychology of Engagement with Everyday life.")

Csikszentmihalyi, M. (1999) Implications of a Systems Perspective for the Study of Creativity. In: Sternberg, R.J. (1999.) (Ed.) Handbook of Creativity. Cambridge: Cambridge University Press.

Csikszentmihalyi, M. (2003) Good Business: Leadership, Flow and the Making of Meaning. New York: Penguin Books.

Dacey, J. S. (1989) Peak Periods of Creative Growth Across the Life-Span. Journal of Creative Behaviour: 1989, Vol. 23 (4), p224 - 247.

Dacey, J.S. and Lennon, K.H. (1998) Understanding Creativity: The Interplay of Biological, Psychological and Social Factors. San Francisco: Jossey-Bass Publishers.

Delcourt, M.A.B. (1993) Creative Productivity Among Secondary School Pupils: Combining Energy, Interest and Imagination. Gifted Child Quarterly. 1993, v37 (1), Winter.

Delcourt: M. (1994) Characteristics of High-Level Creative Productivity: A Longitudinal Study of Students Identified by Renzulli's Three-Ring Conception of Giftedness. In: Subotnik, R.F. and Arnold, K.D. (eds.) (1994.) Beyond Terman: Contemporary Longitudinal Studies of Giftedness and Talent. New Jersey: Ablex Publishing Corporation.

Dennis, W. (1954) Bibliographies of Eminent Scientists. Scientific Monthly. 1954, Vol. 79, p180 - 183.

Domino, G. (1979) Creativity and the Home Environment. Gifted Child Quarterly. Winter 1979, v23(4).

Eliot, T.S. (1944 and 2000) Four Quartets. London, Faber and Faber Ltd.

Erikson, E.H.   (1958 & 1980)   Identity and the Life Cycle.   New York: Norton.

Feldman, D.H., Csikszentmihalyi, M., and Gardner, H.   (1994)   Changing the World: A Framework for the Study of Creativity.   London: Praeger.

Feldman, D.H., Csikszentmihalyi, M., and Gardner, H.   (1994a)   A Framework for the Study of Creativity.   In: Feldman, D.H., Csikszentmihalyi, M., and Gardner, H.   (1994.)   Changing the World: A Framework for the Study of Creativity.   London: Praeger.

Feist, G.J.   (1999)   The Influence of Personailty on Artistic and Scientific Creativity.   In: Sternberg, R.J. (Ed.) (1999).   The Handbook of Creativity.   Cambridge: Cambridge University Press.

Gardner, H. (1988) Creative Lives and Creative works: A Synthetic Approach.   In Sternberg, R.J. (Ed.) The Nature of Creativity. Cambridge: Cambridge University Press.

Gardner, H. (1995) Creating Minds. New York: Basic Books.

Gardner, H.   (1994)   The Creators Patterns.   In: Feldman, D.H., Csikszentmihalyi, M., and Gardner, H.   (1994.)   Changing the World: A Framework for the Study of Creativity.   London: Praeger.

Gardner, H.   (1999)   Intelligence Reframed: Multiple Intelligences for the 21st Century.   New York: Basic books.

Gardner, H.   (2006)   Five Minds for the Future.   Harvard: Harvard Business School press.

Gardner, H. and Moran, J.   (1990)   Family Adaptability, Cohesion and Creativity.   Creativity Research Journal.   1990, v3, pt 4, p281 – 286.

Gardner, H. and Wolf, C.   (1994)   The Fruits of Asynchrony: A Psychological Examination of Creativity.   In: Feldman, D.H., Csikszentmihalyi, M., and Gardner, H.   (1994.)   Changing the World: A Framework for the Study of Creativity.   London: Praeger.

Gedo, J.E. and Gedo, M.M.   (1992)   Perspectives on Creativity: The Biographical Method. Norwood, New Jersey: Ablex Publishing Corporation.

Goertzel, V. and Goertzel, M.G.   (1962)   Cradles of Eminence.   London: Constable.

Goertzel, M.G., Goertzel, V. and Goertzel, T.G.   (1978)   Three Hundred Eminent Personalities. San Francisco: Josey Bass.

Gould, R.   (1972)   The Phases of Adult Life: A Study in Developmental Psychology.   American Journal of Psychiatry.   1972, Vol. 129, p521 – 531.

Gould, R.   (1978)   Transformations: Growth and Change in Adult Life.   New York: Simon and Schuster Ltd.

Gould, R.   (1979)   Transformations in Mid-Life.   1979, Vol. 10, part 2, p2 – 9.

Gruber, H.E. and Wallace, D.B.   (1999)   The Case Study Method and Evolving Systems Approach for Understanding Unique Creative People at Work.   In: Sternberg, R.J.   (1999.)   (Ed.) Handbook of Creativity.   Cambridge: Cambridge University Press.

Guilford, J.P.   (1950) Creativity. American Psychologist.   1950, Vol. 5, p444 - 454.   Republished in Isaksen, S.G.   (Ed.)   (1987)   Frontiers of Creativity Research: Beyond the Basics.   Buffalo, New York: Bearly Ltd.

Helson, R.   (1987) Which of Those Young Women with Creative Potential Became Productive?: From College to Midlife.   In: Hogan, R. and Jones, W.H.   (1987.)   (Eds.) Perspectives in Personality: A Research Annual.   Volume 2: 1987.   London: JAI Press Inc.

Helson, R.   (1999)   A Longitudinal Study of Creative Personality in Women.   Creativity Research Journal.   1999, Vol. 12, pt 2, p89 – 101.

Helson, R. and Moane, G.   (1987)   Personality Change in Women From College to Midlife. Journal of Personality and Social Psychology.   1987, Vol. 53, No. 1, p176 – 186.

Hillman, J.   (1999)   The Force of Character and the Lasting Life.   New York, Random House.

Hunter, S. and Sundel, M.   (Eds.)   (1989)   Midlife Myths: Issues, Findings and Practice Implications.   London: Sage Publications.

Jaques, E.   (1965)   Death and the Mid-Life Crisis.   International Journal of Psychoanalysis. 1965, Vol 46, p502 - 514.

John-Steiner, V.   (1997)   Notebooks of the Mind: Explorations of Thinking.   (Revised Edition). Oxford: Oxford University Press.

Jung, C.G.   (1933)   Modern Man in Search of a Soul.   London: Routledge, Keegan and Paul.

Kanigel, R.   (1986) Apprentice to Genius: The making of a scientific dynasty.   John Hopkins University Press.

Kastenbaum, R.   (1992)   The Creative Process: A Life-Span Approach.   In: Cole, T.R., Van Tassel, D.D., and Katenbaum, R. (Eds.)   Handbook of the Humanities and Aging.   New York: Spinger Publishing Company.

Kaufman, J.C. and Baer, J. (2004) Hawking's Haiku, Madonna's Math: Why It Is Hard to Be Creative in Every Room of the House. In: Sternberg, R.J., Grigorenko, E.L., and Singer, J.L. (Eds.) (2004.) Creativity: From Potential to Realization. Washington DC: American Psychological Association.

Kavaler-Adler, S. (1991) Emily Dickenson – and the Subject of Seclusion. American Journal of Psychoanalysis. 1991, Vol. 51, Pt. 1, p21 – 38.

Kavaler - Adler, S. (1992) The Aging Decline of Two Untreated Border-line Geniuises. Psychoanalysis and Psychotherapy: 1992, Spr. - Sum, Vol. 10 (1), p77 - 100.

Keinanen, M., and Gardner, H. (2004) Vertical and horizontal mentoring. In: Sternberg, R., Grigorenko, E.L, and Singer, J.L. (Eds). (2004). Creativity: From potential to realisation. Washington D.C.; American Psychological Association.

Kets De Vries, M.F.R. (1978) The Midcareer Conundrum. Organizational Dynamics. 1978, Vol. 7, p45 – 62.

Keyes, C.L.M. and Ryff, C.D. (1999) Psychological Well-Being in Midlife. In: Willis, S.L. and Reid, J.D. (1999.) (Eds.) Life in the Middle: Psychological and Social Development in Middle Age. London: Academic Press.

Landau, E. and Moaz, B. (1978) Creativity and Self-actualization in the Ageing Personality. American Journal of Psychotherapy. 1978, Vol. 32, p117 – 127.

Levinson, D.J., Darrow, C.N., Klein, E.B., Levinson, M.H., McKee, B. (1978) The Seasons of a Man's Life. New York: Ballantine Books.

Levinson, D.J., (1986) A Conception of Adult Development. American Psychologist. 1986, Vol 41 (1), p3 - 13.

Levinson, D.J., and Levinson, J. (1996) The Seasons of a Woman's Life. New York, Alfred Knopf Publishers.

Lindauer, M.S. (1992) Creativity in Aging Artists: Contributions from the Humanities to the Psychology of Old Age. Creativity Research Journal. 1992, Vol. 5, 3, p211 - 231.

Lindauer, M.S. (1993) The Span of Creativity Among Long-lived Artists. Creativity Research Journal. 1993, Vol. 6, 3, p221 - 239.

Lindauer, M.S. (1993a) The Old-Age Style and Its Artists. Empirical Study of Aesthetics. 1993, Vol. 11, p135 - 146.

Lindauer, M.S., Orwoll, L. and Kelley, M.C. (1997) Aging Artists on the Creativity of Their Old Age. Creativity Research Journal. 1997, Vol. 10, Pt 2 and 3, p133 – 152.

Loye, D. (2007) Telling the New Story: Darwin, Evolution and Creativity Versus Conformity in Science. In: Richards, R. (Ed.) (2007) Everyday Creativity and New Views of Human Nature; Psychological, Social and Spiritual Perspectives. Washington DC: American Psychological Association.

Lubart, T.I. (1999) Creativity Across Cultures. In: Sternberg, R.J. (Ed.) (1999). The Handbook of Creativity. Cambridge: Cambridge University Press.

Lumsden, C.J. (1999) Evolving Creative Minds: Stories and Mechanisms. In: Sternberg, R.J. (Ed.) (1999). The Handbook of Creativity. Cambridge: Cambridge University Press.

Manheim, A.R. (1998) The Relationship Between the Artistic Process and Self-Actualization. Art Therapy. 1998, Vol. 15, pt 2, p99 – 106.

Martindale, C. (1999). Biological Bases of Creativity. In: Sternberg, R.J. (Ed.) (1999). The Handbook of Creativity. Cambridge: Cambridge University Press.

Maslow, A. (1968) Towards a Psychology of Being. New York: Van Nostran Reinhold.

Maslow, A. (1970) Motivation and Personality: Third edition. London: Harper Collins.

McAdams, D.P. (1993) The Stories We Live By: Personal Myths and the Making of the Self. New York: William Morrow and Company Inc.

McCurdy, H.G. (1957) The Childhood Patterns of Genius. Journal of the Elisha Mitchell Science Society. 1957, Vol. 73, p448 - 462.

McIlroy, J.H. (1984) Midlife in the 1980s: Philosophy, Economy and Psychology. The Personnel and Guidance Journal. 1984, Vol. 62, Part 10, p623 – 628.

Moen, P. and Wethington, E. (1999) Midlife Development in a Life Course Context. In: Willis, S.L. and Reid, J.D. (1999) (Eds.) Life in the Middle: Psychological and Social Development in Middle Age. London: Academic Press.

Munsterberg, H. (1984) The Crown of Life: Artistic Creativity in old Age. London: Harcourt Brace.

Murphy, J.P., Dauw, D.C., Horton, R.E. and Fredian, A.J. (1976) Self-actualisation and Creativity. Journal of Creative Behaviour. 1976, Vol. 10, Pt 1, p39 – 44.

Nakamura, J. and Csikszentmihalyi, M. (2003) Creativity in later life. In: Creativity and Development: Counterpoints – Cognition, Memory and Language. Oxford: Oxford University Press.

Nakamura, J. and Csikszentmihalyi, M. (2005) The Concept of Flow. In: Snyder, C.R. and Lopez, S.J. (Eds.) (2005) Handbook of Positive Psychology. Oxford: Oxford University Press.

Neugarten, B.L. (1969) Continuities and Discontinuities of Psychological Issues Into Adult Life. Human Development. 1969, Vol. 12, p121 – 130.

Neugarten, B.L. (1976) Adaptation and the Life Cycle. Counselling Psychologist. 1976, Vol. 6, p16 – 20.

Neugarten, B.L. (1979) Time, Age and the Life Cycle. American Journal of Psychiatry. 1979, Vol. 136, p887 – 894.

Ochse, R. (1990) Before the Gates of Excellence: The Determinants of Creative genius. Cambridge: Cambridge University Press.

Oles, P.K. (1999) Towards a Psychological Model of the Midlife Crisis. Psychological Reports. 1999, Vol. 84 (3, Pt 2), June 1999, p1059 – 1069.

Policastro, E. and Gardner, H. (1999) From Case Studies to Robust Generalizations: An Approach to the Study of Creativity. In: Sternberg, R.J. (1999) (Ed.) Handbook of Creativity. Cambridge: Cambridge University Press.

Plucker, J.A. and Beghetto, R.A. (2004) Why Creativity Is Domain General, Why It Looks Domain Specific, and Why The Distinction Doesn't Matter. In: Sternberg, R.J., Grigorenko, E.L., and Singer, J.L. (Eds.) (2004) Creativity: From Potential to Realization. Washington DC: American Psychological Association.

Quadrio, C. (1986) The Middle Years. Australian and New Zealand Journal of Family Therapy, 1986, Vol. 7 (1), p33 - 37.

Quenk, N. (1994) Beside Ourselves. California: Consulting Psychologists Press.

Reid, J.D. and Willis, S.L. (1999) Middle Age: New Thoughts, New Directions. In: Willis, S.L. and Reid, J.D. (1999) (Eds.) Life in the Middle: Psychological and Social Development in Middle Age. London: Academic Press.

Richards, R. (Ed.) (2007) Everyday Creativity and New Views of Human Nature; Psychological, Social and Spiritual Perspectives. Washington DC: American Psychological Association.

Richards, R. (2007a) Introduction to Everyday Creativity and New Views of Human Nature; Psychological, Social and Spiritual Perspectives. Washington DC: American Psychological Association.

Richards, R. (2007b) Everyday Creativity: Our Hidden Potential. In: Everyday Creativity and New Views of Human Nature; Psychological, Social and Spiritual Perspectives. Washington DC: American Psychological Association.

Roe, A. (1951) A Psychological Study of Eminent Biologists. Psychological Monographs: General and Applied. 1951, Volume 65, Number 14.

Roe, A. (1951a) A Psychological Study of Physical Scientists. Genetic Psychology Monographs. 1951, May, Volume 43.

Roe, A. (1953) The Making of a Scientist. New York: Dodd, Mead and Company.

Roe, A. (1972) Maintenance of Creative Output Through the Years. In Taylor, C.W. (1972) Climate for Creativity. New York: Pergamon Press.

Rogers, C. (1961) On Becoming a Person. London: Constable & Co.

Rogers, C. (1980 / 2007) The Basic Conditions of the Facilitative Therapeutic Relationship. (Edited version of a talk given at the Medical Facility of the University of Vienna, April 2nd 1981.) In: Cooper, M., O'Hara, M., Schmid, P.F. and Wyatt, G. (Eds). (2007) The Handbook of Person Centred Psychotherapy and Counselling. Basingstoke, Palgrave MacMillan.

Rosenberg, S.D., Rosenberg, H.J. and Farrell, M.P. (1999) The Midlife Crisis Revisited. In: Willis, S.L. and Reid, J.D. (1999) (Eds.) Life in the Middle: Psychological and Social Development in Middle Age. London: Academic Press.

Runco, M.A. (2007) To Understand Is to Create: An Epistemological Perspective on Human Nature and Personal Creativity. In: Richards, R. (Ed.) (2007) Everyday Creativity and New Views of Human Nature; Psychological, Social and Spiritual Perspectives. Washington DC: American Psychological Association.

Ryff, C. (1982) Successful Aging: A Developmental Approach. The Gerontologist. 1982, Vol. 22, pt 2, p209 – 214.

Ryff, C. (1984) Personality Development from the Inside: The Subjective Experience of Change in Adulthood and Aging. In: Baltes, P.B. and Brim, O.G. (Eds.) (1984.) Life Span Development and Behaviour – Volume 6. New York: Academic Press.

Ryff, C. (1989) In the Eye of the Beholder: Views of Psychological Well-Being Among Middle-Aged and Older Adults. Psychology and Aging. 1989, Vol. 4, Pt 2, p195 – 210.

Ryff, C. (1991) Possible Selves in Adulthood and Old Age: A Tale of Shifting Horizons. Psychology and Aging. 1991, Vol. 6, Pt 2, p286 – 295.

Ryff, C. and Heincke, S G. (1983) Subjective Organisation of Personality in Adulthood and Aging. Journal of Personality and Social Psychology. 1983, Vol. 44, pt 4, p807 – 816.

Ryff, C. and Essex, M.J. (1992) The Interpretation of Life Experience and Well-Being: The Sample Case of Relocation. Psychology and Aging. 1992, v7, Pt 4, p507 – 517.

Salthouse, T.A. (1991) Cognitive Facets of Aging Well. Generations. 1991, Vol. 15, Pt. 1, (Winter.)

Ruth, J.E. and Kenyon, G.M. (1996) Biography in Adult Development and Aging. In: Birren, J.E., Kenyon, G.M., Ruth, J.E., Schroots, J.J.F., and Svensson, T. (1996.) (Eds.) Aging and Biography: Explorations in Adult Development. London: Springer Publishing Company.

Sanders, P. (2007) Introduction to the Theory of Person centred Therapy. In: Cooper, M., O'Hara, M., Schmid, P.F. and Wyatt, G. (Eds). (2007) The Handbook of Person Centred Psychotherapy and Counselling. Basingstoke, Palgrave MacMillan.

Sasser - Coen, J. (1993) Qualitative Changes in Creativity in the Second Half of Life: A Life-Span Developmental Perspective. The Journal of Creative Behaviour: 1993, Vol 27 (1), p18 - 27.

Sawyer, R.K. (2006) Explaining Creativity: The Science of Human Innovation. Oxford: Oxford University Press.

Schaie, K.W. (1989) The Hazards of Cognitive Aging. The Gerontologist. 1989, p484 - 493.

Schaie, K.W. (1994) The Course of Adult Intellectual Development. American Psychologist. 1994, Vol. 49 (4), p304 - 313.

Simonton, D.K. (1978) The Eminent Genius in History: The Critical Role of Creative Development. Gifted Child Quarterly. Summer 1978, Vol. 22, p187 - 195.

Simonton, D.K. (1983) Dramatic Greatness and Content: a Quantitative Study of 82 Athenian and Shakespearean plays. Empirical Studies of the Arts. 1983, Vol. 1, p109 - 123.

Simonton, D.K. (1983a) Formal Education, Eminence and Dogmatism. Journal of Creative Behaviour: 1983: Vol. 17, p149 - 162.

Simonton. D.K. (1983b) Intergenerational Transfer of Individual Differences in Hereditary Monarchs: Genetic, Role-Modeling, Cohort, or Sociocultural Effects? Journal of Personality and Social Psychology. 1983, Vol. 44, part 2, p354 - 364.

Simonton, D.K. (1984c) Popularity, Content and Context in 37 Shakespeare plays. Poetics. 1986, Vol. 15, p493 – 510.

Simonton, D.K. (1990) Does creativity decline in later years? Definition, data and theory. In: Perlmutter, M. (Ed.) Late Life Potential Washington: The Gerontological Society of America.

Simonton, D.K. (1990a) Creativity and Wisdom in Aging. In Birren, J.E. and Schaie, K.W. (Eds.) Handbook of the Psychology of Aging (Third Edition). London: Academic press Inc.

Simonton, D.K. (1990b) Creativity in the Later Years: Optimistic Prospects for Achievement. The Gerontologist. 1990, Vol. 30, 5, p626 - 631.

Simonton, D.K. (1991) Creative Productivity Through The Adult Years. Generations. 1991, p13 - 16.

Simonton, D.K (1994) Greatness: Who Makes History and Why. New York: Guilford Press Inc.

Simonton, D.K. (1995) Exceptional Personal Influence: An Integrative Paradigm. Creativity Research Journal. 1995, Vol. 8, pt 4, p371 – 376.

Simonton, D.K (1997) Genius and Creativity: Selected Papers. Connecticut: Ablex Publishing Corporation.

Simonton, D.K. (1997a) Creative Productivity: A Predictive and Explanatory Model of Career Trajectories and Landmarks. Psychological Review. 1997, Vol. 104, pt 1, p66 – 89.

Simonton, D.K. (1999) Creativity from a Historiometric Perspective. In: Sternberg, R.J. (1999.) (Ed.) Handbook of Creativity. Cambridge: Cambridge University Press.

Simonton, D.K. (1999a) Origins of Genius: Darwinian Perspectives on Creativity. Oxford: Oxford University Press.

Simonton, D.K. (1999b) Talent and Its Development: An Emergenic and Epigenetic Model. Psychological Review. 1999. VOL. 106, pt 3, p435 – 457.

Simpson, E.L. (1980) Occupational Endeavour as Life History: Anne Roe. Psychology of Women Quarterly. 1980, Vol. 5, pt 1, p116 – 126.

Snyder, C.R. and Lopez, S.J. (Eds.) (2005) Handbook of Positive Psychology. Oxford: Oxford University Press.

Stein, M. (1983) In the Midlife. Dallas Tx: Spring Publications.

Sternberg, R.J. (Ed.) (1999) The Handbook of Creativity. Cambridge: Cambridge University Press.

Sternberg, R.J., Grigorenko, E.L., and Singer, J.L. (Eds.) (2004) Creativity: From Potential to Realization. Washington DC: American Psychological Association.

Sternberg, R.J., Kaufman, J.C., and Grigorenko, E.L. (2008) Applied Intelligence. Cambridge: Cambridge University Press.

Stevens, A. and Price, J. (2000) Evolutionary Psychiatry: A new beginning. (Second Edition.) London: Routledge.

Storr, A. (1988) The School of Genius. London: Andre Deutsch.

Storr, A. (1989) Churchill's Black Dog – and Other Phenomena of the Human Mind. London: Harper Collins Publishers.

Subotnik, R.F. and Steiner, C.L. (1994) Adult Manifestations of Talent in Science: A Longitudinal Study of 1983 Westinghouse Science Talent Search Winners. In: Subotnik, R.F. and Arnold, K.D. (eds.) (1994) Beyond Terman: Contemporary Longitudinal Studies of Giftedness and Talent. New Jersey: Ablex Publishing Corporation.

Subotnik, R.F. and Arnold, K.D. (1994a) Longitudinal Studies of Giftedness and Talent. In: Subotnik, R.F. and Arnold, K.D. (eds.) (1994) Beyond Terman: Contemporary Longitudinal Studies of Giftedness and Talent. New Jersey: Ablex Publishing Corporation.

Subotnik, R.F. and Steiner, C.L. (1994) Adult Manifestations of Talent in Science: A Longitudinal Study of 1983 Westinghouse Science Talent Search Winners. In: Subotnik, R.F. and Arnold, K.D. (eds.) (1994) Beyond Terman: Contemporary Longitudinal Studies of Giftedness and Talent. New Jersey: Ablex Publishing Corporation.

Torrance, E.P. (1963) The Creative Potential of School Children in the Space Age. (Reprinted in: Torrance, E.P. (1995) Why Fly?: A Philosophy of Creativity. New Jersey: Ablex Publishing Corporation.)

Torrance, E.P. (1986) The Dangers of Being a Creative Teacher - The Dangers in Challenging Students to be Creative. Originally an unpublished paper given at the University of Massachusetts, Amherst. (Subsequently published in: Torrance, E.P. (1995) Why Fly?: A Philosophy of Creativity. New Jersey: Ablex Publishing Corporation.)

Torrance, E.P. (1995) Why Fly?: A Philosophy of Creativity. New Jersey: Ablex Publishing Corporation.

Vaillant, G.E. (1977) Adaptation to Life. Boston: Little, Brown and Co.

Vaillant, G.E. (1993) Wisdom and the Ego. Cambridge: Harvard University Press.

Walters, J. and Gardner, H. (1986) The Crystillizing Experience: Discovering an Intellectual Gift. In: Sternberg, R.J. and Davidson, J. (Eds.) Conceptions of Giftedness. Cambridge: Cambridge University Press.

Walters, J. and Gardner, H. (1992) The Crystallizing Experience: Discovering and Intellectual Gift. In: Albert, R.S. (Ed.) (1992). Genius and Eminence (Second Edition). Oxford: Pergamon Press.

Walberg, H.J., Rasher, S.P., and Parkerson, J. (1980) Childhood and Eminence. Journal of Creative Behaviour: 1980, Vol. 13, p225 - 231.

Willis, S.L. and Reid, J.D. (1999) (Eds.) Life in the Middle: Psychological and Social Development in Middle Age. London: Academic Press.

Wolf, M. A. (1991) The Discovery of Middle Age: An Educational Task in Training Gerontologists. Educational Gerontology: 1991, Nov - Dec, Vol. 17 (6), p559 - 571.

Wolf, N. (2006) The Tree House. London: Virago Press

Wyatt- Brown, A.M. (1988) Late Life Style in the Novels of Barbera Pym and Penelope Mortimer. The Gerontologist. 1988, Vol. 28, Pt 6, p835 – 839.

Zuckerman, H. (1977) The Scientific Elite: Nobel Laureates' Mutual Influences. Reprinted in: Albert, R. S. (Ed.) (1992) Genius and Eminence. Oxford: Pergamon Press. (Second edition.)

End Notes

Chapter 1

1   I am following at academic convention in using the word 'domain' to describe a body of knowledge and an area of skill about a single topic.
2   (e.g. Maslow 1970)
3   (ibid.: p61)
4   (ibid.: p126)
5   (Maslow 1968: p155)
6   (Maslow 1970: p56)
7   (Bohart 2007: p48)
8   (Maslow 1970: p126)
9   (Csikszentmihalyi 1992: p10)
10 (Sanders 2007: p13)
11 (Csikszentmihalyi 1992: p221)
12 (Csikszentmihalyi 1993: p219)
13 (Compton 2005: p12/15). 'Eudaimonia' is an idea that relates back to the philosopher Aristotle, and the suggestion that a life led a certain way is supportive of happiness.
14 See references at the end of the book.
15 (Maslow 1970: p127)
16 (Maslow 1968: p155)
17 (Maslow 1970: p128)
18 (Bohart 2007: p48)
19 (Maslow 1970: p142)
20 (Sanders 2007: p12)
21 The definition of self-actualising creativeness appears to overlap with that of 'everyday creativity' proposed by Ruth Richards (2007) and explored later in this chapter.
22 (Murphy et al 1976: p39)
23 (Craft 2000)
24 (Manheim 1998: p101)
25 (after Rhodes 1961)
26 (Barron 1988: p80)

27   (Sawyer 2006)

28   This argument or polarity in literature appears to have lessened in recent years, with an acceptance of domain-specific and everyday creativity.   However, it still recurs.

29   (Worth 2000; Plucker and Beghetto 2004; Richards 2007, 2007a, 2007b; Loye 2007)

30   (Sawyer 2006: p6/7)

31   (E.g. Gardner 2006: p81; Sternberg et al 2008: p291)

32   (Gardner 1995 and 2006)

33   (Kaufman and Baer 2004: p9)

34   (Richards 2007a: p7)

35   Both writing in 2007.

36   (Richards 2007a: p3)

37   (ibid: p6).

38   (ibid: p12).

39   (ibid: p13).

40   (ibid: p27).

41   (Loye 2007).

42   (Runco 2004: p22 ; 2007: p92 – 4).

43   (ibid: p97).

44   (ibid: p99).

45   (Kaufman and Baer 2004: p5).

46   (ibid: p6).

47   (Plucker and Beghetto 2004: p156)

48   (Amabile 1996. Craft 2000. Csikszentmihalyi 1997a. Feldman et al 1994. Freeman 1993. Gardner 1999a. Maslow 1970. Richards 2007. Worth 2000.)

49   (Feldman 1994).

50   (Csikszentmihalyi 1997).

51   (Craft 2000).

52   (Freeman 1993).

53   (Gardner 1999).

54   (Csikszentmihalyi 1999: p313)

55   (E.g. Freeman 1993: p10, Winner 2000.)

56   (E.g. Csikszentmihalyi 1988)

57   (Sternberg and Lubart 1999: p12)

58   (Csikszentmihalyi 1996: p23)

59   (Csikszentmihalyi 1999: p314)

60   (Gardner 2006: p3)

61   (Simonton 1983a: p150; Albert 1992a: p7)

62   (Csikszentmihalyi 1996: p27)

63   (Gardner 2006: p81)

64   (Csikszentmihalyi 1988: p326 and Ochse 1990: p57)

65   (Csikszentmihalyi 1988: p329 and 333)

66   (Feldman 1994: p20 and 22; Csikszentmihalyi 1996: p27; Gardner 2006: p80).

67   (Csikszentmihalyi 1988: p330 and 1999: p315).

68   (Csikszentmihalyi 1996: p37).

69   (Feldman 1994: p16)

70   (Csikszentmihalyi 1988: p330 and 1996: p28; Gardner 2006: p80)
71   (Gardner and Wolf 1994: p57/8; Feldman 1994: p16; Csikszentmihalyi 1998: p331, 1996: p28 and 1999: p315, 328 and 329)
72   (Feldman 1994: p36)
73   (Csikszentmihalyi 1999: p322, 3 and 7).
74   (Freeman 1993: p10; Csikszentmihalyi 1996: p47, and 1999: p332).
75   This possibility is taken up in more detail in Chapter 2.
76   (Feldman 1994: p25)
77   (Nakamura and Csikszentmihalyi 2005: p89).
78   For example: chess, surgery, psychiatry, farming, weaving, mountain climbing, sport, music, reading, conversation, poetry, writing and work (ibid: p144 / 148).
79   (ibid: p2 and 48).
80   (ibid: 2005: p90).
81   (ibid: p5).
82   (ibid: p48).
83   (ibid: p49).
84   (ibid p4).
85   (1993: p177).
86   (1992: p150).
87   (Nakamura and Csikszentmihalyi 2005: p89/90)
88   (Csikszentmihalyi 2003: pages 67, 72 and 74 and summarised below).
89   (Csikszentmihalyi 2003: p73)
90   (Csikszentmihalyi 2003: p48).
91   (Nakamura and Csikszentmihalyi 2005: p91).
92   (Policastro and Gardner 1999: p220 - 2).
93   (Gardner 1997: p10–13).
94   (Gardner 1997: p12)
95   (Ghislen 1952).
96   (Csikszentmihalyi 1975: p37; Maslow 1970: p163).
97   (Csikszentmihalyi 1975: p37).
98   (Maslow 1970: p162).
99   (Csikszentmihalyi 1975: p44; 1997: p39).
100   (E.g. Amabile 1983, 1996; Maslow 1970: p60 and 136; Csikszentmihalyi 1990: p3, 1997: p121).

Chapter 2
101   (Sawyer 2006: p306 – 312).
102   (Sawyer 2006: p303)
103   (Wolf 2006: p26).
104   (Walters and Gardner 1992: p135)
105   (Gardner1999: p41 - 43)
106   (Sawyer 2006:p307/8).
107   (Wolf 2006: p218).
108   (Csikszentmihalyi 2003: p73)
109   (Ibid 2003: pages 67, 72 and 74)

110   (Csikszentmihalyi 2003: p48).

111   These questions and guidance draw on the work of Carr 2004: p70.

112   (Compton 2005: p35).

Chapter 3

113   (E.g. Kanigel 1986, Zuckerman 1977.)

114   Different research cites the influence of parents, friends, lovers, peers as well as the older experienced professional in the same field of work.

115   (Levinson 'et al' 1978).

116   (Levinson 1996, e.g. p239).

117   (John-Steiner 1997).

118   (John-Steiner 1997: p41).

119   (Goertzel and Goertzel 1962: p3; Goertzel et al 1978: p13; Ochse 1990: p64; Dacey and Lennon 1998: p53).

120   (Domino 1979: p819-825; Walberg et al 1980: p231; Bloom 1985: p440; Albert 1992: p175; Csikszentmihalyi et al 1993: p7; Csikszentmihalyi 1996: p161).

121   (Bloom 1985).

122   (Delcourt 1993: p26).

123   (Goertzel and Goertzel 1962: p6).

124   (John-Steiner 1997: p41 and 161).

125   (Csikszentmihalyi et al 1993: p173).

126   (Csikszentmihalyi 1996: p163).

127   (Goertzel and Goertzel 1962: p132)

128   (Goertzel et al 1978: p37)

129   (E.g. Goertzel and Goertzel 1962 p241 -4; Torrance 1963: p12; Ochse 1990: p88; Csikszentmihalyi et al 1993: p180-1; Csikszentmihalyi 1996: p173; Dacey and Lennon 1998: ch4.)

130   (Albert 1992a: p12-3; Goertzel and Goertzel 1962: p246; Goertzel et al 1978: p-337; Csikszentmihalyi 1996: p173).

131   (Roe 1951, 1951a, 1953; Walberg et al 1980; Csikszentmihalyi et al 1993: p180-1; Csikszentmihalyi 1996: p173-4).

132   (Torrance 1983: p72-78).

133   (Csikszentmihalyi et al 1993: p184-5).

134   (Torrance 1981: p55; Csikszentmihalyi et al 1993: p188; Csikszentmihalyi 1996: p173-4).

135   (Torrance 1986: p112).

136   (Csikszentmihalyi et al 1993: p177).

137   (Csikszentmihalyi 1992: p29).

138   (Albert 1992a: p15).

139   (Walberg et al 1980: p228-9).

140   (Ochse 1990: p71).

141   (Simonton 1978: p189 and 1983: p354).

142   (Torrance 1961, 1983 and 1995)

143   (Albert 1996: p44, Csikszentmihalyi 1993: ch12).

144   (Goertzel 1978: chapter 12; Albert 1996: p44).

145   (Helson 1987).

146   (Subotnik and Steiner 1994).

147   (John-Steiner 1997: p45).

148   (Albert 1992: p126).

149   (Keinanen and Gardner 2004; pages 171, 189 - 191).

150   Published in 1993 by John Hopkins University Press.

151   (Zuckerman 1977: p159 - 167).

152   (Subotnik and Steiner 1994: p54).

153   (Gardner 1993: p384/5).

154   (Simonton 1983b, 1984c).

155   (Levinson 'et al' 1978: p97 / 8).

156   (Gardner 2001).

157   Vaillant 2002: p114/5

Chapter 4

158   (E.g. Vaillant 1977; Levinson et al 1978; Levinson 1996; Vaillant 2002.)

159   (Chopra 2008: In: Marohn 2008).

160   (Levinson 1978, 1996; Vaillant 1977; Gould 1978; Roazen 1976).

161   (Hunter and Sundel 1989: p8).

162   (Neugarten 1969: p121, Gould 1979: p2).

163   (Levinson 1978, 1996).

164   (Vaillant 1977, 2002.)

165   (E.g. Levinson et al1978 and Levinson 1996).

166   (E.g. Moen and Wethington 1999: p4; Oles 1999: p1059).

167   (Jaques 1965).

168   (E.g. Reid and Willis 1999: p277).

169   (Brim 1976: p4).

170   (Hunter and Sundel 1989: p19).

171   Discussed further overleaf: "A growing exploration and sense of who the individual is as a person, what they want, as well as what the realities of the world and life are really like".

172   (E.g. Moen and Wethington 1999: p21)

173   (Moen and Wethington 1999: p13).

174   (Rosenberg et al 1999: p56).

175   (Vaillant 1977; p219).

176   (Jung 1971; p12).

177   (Brim 1976: p5).

178   (Levinson 1978: p192; Gould 1979: p2; Kets de Vries 1978: p45; McIlroy 1984: p625; Quadrio 1986: p37; McAdams 1993: p198; Levinson 1996: p377).

179   (E.g. Brim 1976: p5; Levinson et al 1978: p200; Kets de vries 1978: p48).

180   (McIlroy 1984: p625).

181   (Kets de Vries 1978: p48; McAdams 1993: p202/3; Vaillant 1977: p202).

182   (Neugarten 1969: p121/2).

183   (Jaques 1965: p506).

184   (Neugarten 1969: p121/2; McIlroy 1984: p625; Quadrio 1986: p34/5).

185   (Gould 1979: p2/3).
186   (Jaques 1965: p507; Neugarten 1969: p97; Brim 1976: p5; Kets de Vries 1978: p47; McIlroy 1984: p625; McAdams 1993: p198).
187   (Jaques 1965: p505).
188   (McAdams 1993: p200).
189   (Gould 1972: p530; Quadrio 1986: p34/5; Reid and Willis 1999: p277).
190   (Moen and Wethington 1999: p14).
191   (Kastenbaum 1992: p291).
192   (Lehman 1953. Simonton 1990, 1990a, 1990b, 1991, 1994, Lindauer 1993).
193   (Simonton 1990b: p629).
194   (E.g. Simonton 1984, 1990, 1991).
195   (Simonton 1990b: p627).
196   (E.g. Dennis 1954).
197   (Simonton 1990: p103; 1990a: p324).
198   (Simonton 1990a: p323; 1991: p15; 1994: p203).
199   (Simonton 1990: p103; 1990b: p627).
200   (McAdams 1993: p202).
201   (Jaques 1965, Pankey 1998.)
202   (Gould 1979: p3).
203   (Jung 1933, Erikson 1958, Levinson 1978, 1986, 1996;, Neugarten 1969, 1976, Quadrio 1986, Quenk 1993 and 1996, Stein 1983; Corlett and Milner 1993).
204   (Ibid: p199).
205   (Ibid: 2003: p200 - 204).
206   (Ibid: 2003: p204).
207   (Ibid: 2003: p205).
208   (Cohen –Shalev 1986 and 1989).
209   (Kastenbaum 1992: p292).
210   (Cohen-Shalev 1989: p33).
211   (Lindauer 1992: p215 - 7).
212   (Munsterberg 1984).
213   (Simonton 1990b: p627).
214   (Examined by Gedo and Gedo 1992: p27).
215   (Simonton 1994).
216   (Cohen-Shalev 1989: p28).
217   (Storr 1988: p169 and 1989: p147)
218   (Vaillant 2002: p224).
219   (Ibid: p213 - 21).
220   (Lindauer et al 1997: p134 - 9).

Index

S

T

V

W

Y

Z